The Religion of
Ethical Nationhood

The Religion of Ethical Nationhood

JUDAISM'S CONTRIBUTION TO WORLD PEACE

by Mordecai M. Kaplan

THE MACMILLAN COMPANY

COLLIER-MACMILLAN LTD., LONDON

To the Memory

of

A H A D H A - A M
(Asher Ginzberg)

who revealed to me the spiritual reality of the Jewish people

of

S O L O M O N S C H E C H T E R
who granted me the opportunity to transmit it to my students

and of

L O U I S D E M B I T Z B R A N D E I S
who pleaded for ethical nationhood in American life

Contents

PREFACE   ix

CHAPTER I

Jewish Religion in a New Key   1

   1. In the Key of Naturalism   1
   2. In the Key of Humanism   8

CHAPTER II

Jewish Religion as Mature Wisdom   19

   1. Group Religion as Experience   19
   2. Demythologizing What Man Means to God   35
   3. What God Means to Man   49

CHAPTER III

Nature's God as the Source of Moral Law   57

CHAPTER IV

What Is Man?   77

   1. What Psychology Can Learn from Religion   77
   2. What Religion Can Learn from Psychology   83
   3. The Human Person   88

CHAPTER V

Man's Sense of Destiny   95

CHAPTER VI

Zionism's Unfinished Business   116

    1. The Need for an Ideology   116
    2. The Reconstitution of the Jewish People   126

CHAPTER VII

American Jewry's Unfinished Business   136

    1. The Communal Organization of American Jewry   136
    2. Judaism's Contribution to American Life   154

CHAPTER VIII

The Problem of Jewish Education in the Diaspora   168

    1. The Communal Responsibility for Jewish Education
    168
    2. New Emphases in Jewish Education   178
    3. The Rabbinic Training for Our Day   187

EPILOGUE   202

Preface

THIS book promulgates the idea of ethical nationhood as the only means of forestalling the doom that threatens human and world survival. Public religion may achieve that purpose if it is demythologized of supernaturalism and otherworldliness.

As now constituted, sovereign nation states cannot cope with the dangers of overpopulation, depletion of resources and nuclear warfare. Mankind's only hope lies in the rise of a spiritual leadership devoted to the eradication of man-made evils.

Absolved of all moral responsibility by their absolute sovereignties, nations seem to be headed for a world holocaust. Can public religion impose ethical limitations upon national sovereignty and foster ethical nationhood? "The major nations are now capable of expunging life from this planet," wrote Norman Cousins. "Force is extolled and endlessly multiplied despite the fact that security no longer depends on the pursuit of force but on the control of force . . .

"We seek to confront the danger by enlarging it and igniting it instead of recognizing that there is now a totally new condition on earth, calling for a new emphasis on world controls and world approaches. The old reflexes of absolute national sovereignty are inconsistent with either peace or progress . . ." (*Saturday Review*, March 8, 1969).

Ancient Israel was the first nation to have come upon the idea of ethical nationhood which it translated into religion.

Embodied in the Torah is the idea that the nation's social, political, economic and military activities should be conducted in the spirit of "justice spelled into law," which is what God should mean to man. In accordance with that spirit, the Jews who are the biological and spiritual descendants of ancient Israel should resume the vocation of fostering ethical nationhood in the contemporary world.

To my gratitude to God for having enabled me to live creatively beyond the Psalmist's reckoning, I wish to add my indebtedness to the Jewish Theological Seminary of America for having granted me the academic freedom to deviate from its theological version of Judaism throughout the well-nigh sixty years of my association with it, and to the Society for the Advancement of Judaism for having made possible the launching of the Reconstructionist movement. My heartfelt thanks go out to Mrs. Marian Greenberg for her perceptive editing of the original text of this book.

MORDECAI M. KAPLAN

The Religion of
Ethical Nationhood

CHAPTER I

Jewish Religion in a New Key

1. IN THE KEY OF NATURALISM

"I left religion during college," wrote Susanne K. Langer, the author of *Philosophy in a New Key*. "When I began to have faith in my mind and my feeling of insecurity disappeared, religion became untenable, and therefore dispensable" (*The New Yorker*, December 3, 1960). Although my own experience as a young Orthodox rabbi was similar, my conclusion was different. While ministering to my congregation, I began to have more faith in my own mind than in the Orthodox Jewish tradition in which I had been educated. But I decided to leave the Orthodox rabbinate, not Judaism. Following the dictates of reason, I conceived of Judaism as the evolving religious civilization of the Jewish people. And ever since I have sought ideological validation of the Jewish people's will to resume its historic role as a "light to the nations."

Since group religion expresses that cosmic drive which impels men and nations toward spirituality and holiness, it fosters the creative survival of the human species and the self-fulfillment of the individual. But group religion cannot raise the ethical standard of men and nations unless it is rooted in the realities of physical and human nature. Its validity must be judged by its effectiveness in securing the emergence of a warless world based on freedom and justice. Viewed as a social phenomenon, group religion is buttressed—not upon what man means to God—but on what God means to man. Only the transposition of Judaism into the new key of naturalism can assure a creative future to the Jewish people.

The spiritual leaders of ancient Israel expressed their intuitions in terms of the primitive world outlook of their times. In keeping with the tendency to thingify or personify general and abstract ideas, the priests, prophets and sages conceived of God in the image of man. They designated the nation which was to live by His laws as His chosen people and they regarded the laws which spelled out justice as having been revealed by God.

Although contemporary Jews acknowledge their descent from and allegiance to the ancient House of Israel, they are pulled by the centrifugal attraction of the open society. How shall modern Jews resolve this inner conflict? Certainly the continued emphasis of traditional religion upon the supernatural nature of the spiritual heritage of the Jewish people will make no sense to the scientifically trained Jew who, even when he affirms the reality of God's existence, feels obliged to assert His unknowability and ineffability. Religion cannot be regarded as tenable, much less indispensable, to modern man unless it is transposed from the key of supernaturalism into the key of naturalism and functionalism. The transposition of traditional Jewish religion into that new key requires an authentic conception of human nature from the standpoint of its needs and satisfactions for creative life.

Paramount in the threefold Jewish spiritual heritage—God, Israel and Torah—is the reality of the people of Israel. But while contemporary Jewry identifies itself with ancient Israel, can it reconstitute itself as an authentic equivalent for that Jewish people which was commanded to serve as a paradigm of ethical nationhood? That vocation is implicit in the divine promise to each of the three Patriarchs through whose descendants "all the nations of the earth shall invoke blessings on themselves." It is reaffirmed in the scripture which exhorts the people of Israel to adhere to the Eternal their God and heed His commands. Thereby they will demonstrate "their wisdom and intelligence to the nations, who, when they hear of all these statutes, will say, 'This great nation is, indeed, a wise and intelligent people' " (Deut. 4:6). Thus the God of history calls upon the Jews to renew their covenant with Him and to foster their solidarity in accordance with the principle of ethical nationhood. This reconstruction of the traditional version of Jewish peoplehood defines the role which the Jews of today should play in the modern world.

Traditional Judaism is the organic synthesis of three realities: the functioning of the belief in the only authentic God, the ancient nation of Israel, and the Torah which God had revealed to it. In the supernaturalist version of that tradition, God is conceived as a being outside and above nature, the nation of Israel is believed to have been chosen by God as an example to other nations of virtue and blessedness, and the Torah consists of a declaration of Israel's dependence on God and a constitution detailing the laws by which the people of Israel is to live.

However, in the words of Ellis Rivkin:

> We are now in an age of dynamic and rapid transformation, an age in which innovation and change are the norm. Ushered in by technology, with capitalism as its primary force, ours is an age of permanent revolution. In this age, religious systems committed to unchanging traditions are doomed to irrelevance and Judaism exists today because it has built within its concept of the one God the dynamic for change and development ["The Age of Permanent Revolution," *Dimensions*, Vol III, Winter 2, 1968–69, p. 8].

Zionism has demonstrated that human initiative, rather than divine intervention, established the Jewish State. But, obsessed with the monumental tasks of land settlement and reclamation, human rescue and rehabilitation, polity and defense, Zionism was in no position to formulate a comprehensive program for restructuring the Jewish people. Time is running out. The Jewish people must be reconstituted. A practicable program for its creative survival as a transnational people—with the Jewish community in the State of Israel as a catalytic agent for the rest of Jewry—must be implemented.

The realization of that goal depends in large measure upon the reinterpretation of the belief in God in terms compatible with a naturalist world outlook. Thereby Judaism may revitalize those, particularly the youth, who have become alienated because of its traditional supernaturalism. The term "God" belongs to the category of *functional* nouns. Gold, silver, wood, are *substantive* nouns, but teacher, shepherd, king, are *functional* nouns. A functional noun is necessarily correlative: one is a teacher of a pupil, a shepherd of a herd, king or God of a people.

In his *Guide for the Perplexed*, Maimonides, who had no conception of function, declared: "No definition can be given of God." But in the Bible, the word *Elohim* (God) unmistakably refers to the way He functions. Thus we read: "Hear O Israel, YHWH *is* our God," which means YHWH functions as God. Likewise: "I YHWH am your God, who brought you out of the land of Egypt to *be* your God" (Num. 15:41). God's function is analogous to that of a king who decrees and administers laws. Hence in every benediction God is referred to as the King of the universe. In other words, "God" as a functional term denotes a relationship of supreme importance to a people or to mankind. This radically different approach stresses what God means to mankind. It rejects the ideationist approach of theological writings which deal with what God *is* instead of what He *does*.

The functional view of religion and its problems also differs (1) from the revelational approach based on supernaturalism, (2) from the idealist notion (Platonic) that only what is static is immutable and authentic, and (3) from the ideationist approach (Aristotelian) which dichotomizes experience into contrasting categories such as body versus mind, substance versus attributes, and so on. The transcendental approach (Kantian) postulates the dualism of pure versus practical reason.

Functionalism deprecates all ontological dualisms, whether of the cosmos or of the human mind. Since its main concern in understanding reality is to improve it, functionalism deals with the relation of means to ends and sheds light upon the *purpose* and *meaning* of human experience. Applied to Jewish experience, the method of functional rationalism reveals Judaism as not merely a system of religious beliefs and practices, but as the sum of all those manifestations of the Jewish people's will to live creatively. Thus viewed, Judaism is nothing less than an evolving religious civilization.

Judaism functions as a way of life, in which *peoplehood*, *religion* and *culture* are so intertwined as to be incapable of being dealt with separately. Each aspect loses value when treated in isolation. The interrelatedness of the Jewish idea of God, Israel and Torah is expressed in the mystic aphorism, "The Holy One, blessed be He, Israel and the Torah are a unity." Judaism has become a problem because the Jewish people is in a state of crisis. The security of its homeland, the reconstitution of its disintegrating body, and the recovery of its faith in the spiritual significance of its will to live can revitalize the Jewish people.

Man's concept of reality derives from something seen, heard, felt, inferred, believed or assumed. It proceeds from the known to the unknown. In the past, religions based belief in God upon *traditions* concerning His self-revelation through visions and oracles. Those traditions are now discounted by all who have become habituated to scientific thought. Although scientifically oriented people form a small minority of mankind, their influence is bound to increase. In time their rejection of the *traditional* basis of the belief in God will be emulated by the masses.

Traditional beliefs and practices must be reinterpreted in the light of understandable and communicable experience which does not hide behind the cloud of mystifying paradoxes. Even paradox must reflect universal experience and not private mystery. For example, moral freedom can be proved to be as much of a paradox as Zeno proved motion to be. The intelligent person will reject a religion if it lays claim to operate at its deepest level in a mystic no-mind's-land.

The thought pattern underlying any effort to revitalize traditional religion must be an empirical and verifiable version of human experience. It would have to single out, from the standpoint of faith in human improvability, that which is common to all religions. It would view each religion as a way of life *shared by a group* which accepts some common goal for attaining salvation. The adherents of such group religions must be aware of themselves as constituting a people, nation, church or fellowship.

This Copernican revolution in religious thought proceeds from the assumption that the central element in religion is not its idea of God but of salvation. *Whatever constitutes salvation for the religious community determines the idea of God which the religion of that community professes.*

Since every one of the historical religions is in a state of crisis, there must be something wrong with what they teach concerning man's salvation. Conceived in supernatural context, salvation is an act of Divine Grace in whose hands the origin and destiny of the human soul lie. God may deal with the soul arbitrarily or miraculously. But man's implicit belief in that primitive conception of salvation has redemptive power; its rejection commits the sinner to eternal damnation. Should modern man repudiate all aspects of traditional religions because of these supernaturalist beliefs? Those who have a sense of history and of social and spiritual continuity will try to conserve the permanent values of traditional religions—that supreme good which for them represents salvation.

Stripped of supernaturalism, the ethical trends of the historical religions would articulate more clearly that which is an authentically supreme good. Those ethical trends as well as theologies and rituals would take on new meaning and function once more as instruments of spiritual fellowship and communion. Relinquishing monopolistic claims to salvation, religions would reflect the progressive and spiritual aspirations of their respective adherents; they would recognize the validity of other religions. Mankind stands in need of spiritual values based on a conception of human destiny for the individual and society which will augment the measure of integrity, responsibility, loyalty, love, courage and creativity in human affairs and which will enable man to attain the full measure of humanity and God-likeness.

Even though that purpose may not be achieved within the foreseeable future, that is no reason for ascribing such failure to original sin or to the inherent depravity of man. The concept of original sin based on the book of Genesis conveys the traditional version of the nature of man. Emancipation from the authority of that text makes possible the substitution of a more constructive view of human nature as capable of improvement. Through continuous growth and progressive approximation to the ideal, mankind may achieve self-fulfillment and salvation.

This striving for self-improvement may so transform the human being as virtually to effect his metamorphosis. Unlike other living creatures, man takes a hand in his own metamorphosis and contributes his share to the cosmic process which impels him to become fully human. His impulse to make the best use of life, which derives from the transcendent and divine, involves reliance upon the creative insights of the great historical religions. *In the process of reconstructing them, man will mold his character and organize his life rationally and spiritually.*

A religion should foster man's integrity, responsibility, loyalty, love, courage and creativity. *The achievement of those traits on a personal and social scale constitutes man's fulfillment or salvation.* Insofar as human nature is an integral part of the cosmos, a functional conception of God depends upon the knowledge of human nature from the standpoint of those moral and spiritual traits. In religion, as in other aspects of human life, faith in tradition and blind obedience to authority should give way to reasoned experience and confidence in man's moral responsibility.

To become once again a vital force in human life religion should renounce all magic or theurgy and should reinforce man's efforts to better his own nature as well as his social and physical environment. The belief in God can answer man's unanswerable questions. It should underpin his faith in that continuous self-improvement which parallels creativity in the cosmos. This new development in religion marks the latest stage in the evolution of man. His capacity to play a conscious and responsible role in his own evolution manifests his creative freedom. This naturalist interpretation of the traditional teaching that man was made in the image of God regards man as co-worker with God and as artist of his own life.

The field in which man fashions his life is multi-dimensional. It consists of (1) the life substance given at birth, together with the environmental conditions that sustain it through the actualization of potentialities; (2) the purposes that give direction to man's efforts; (3) the spiritual values which embody those purposes; and (4) the means, instruments and agencies through which those purposes are to be achieved. Each dimension of human life has its own set of values. Man's artistry, which calls for lifelong education and practice, consists in so combining and organizing the values in all those dimensions as to produce a harmonious personality and a cooperative society.

These principles, studied in their relation to one another and in their operation in actual life, might form the basis of a science to be known as *Soterics*, a term derived from the Greek noun *soteria*, which means salvation. Soterics might well serve as a method of formulating the theoretic aspect of the art of living. With the help of God, the Cosmic Spirit that impels man ever to transcend himself, man might learn to utilize the forces of nature for his salvation instead of for his annihilation. To invoke and activate that help should be the function of every institutional religion which seeks to make the world safe for man and man safe for the world. To accomplish that end *religion* must be set in a new key, the key of naturalism.

2. IN THE KEY OF HUMANISM

At a symposium, reported in the Spring 1965 issue of *Jewish Heritage*, leading Jewish intellectuals testified that Judaism was becoming irrelevant to increasing numbers of Jews and that the Jewish people had nothing to contribute to contemporary spiritual values. Only the professional Jew, they asserted, cherishes loyalty to his people as an end in itself.

Can Zionism guarantee a future to Judaism and the Jewish people? Even if one discounts Arab terrorism and threats of annihilation—as well as the hostility on theological grounds of certain Christian circles to the State of Israel—there remain manifold internal dangers to meaningful survival. After a year's research in Israel the French sociologist Georges Friedmann arrived at the ominous verdict suggested in his title *The End of the Jewish People?* (English edition, 1965). He characterized first- and second-generation Israelis as motivated by "action without ideology, marked by an indifference to all spiritual values." In Friedmann's view, Israeli condescension toward diaspora Jews discourages reliance on a pragmatic and secular Israel for both the renaissance of Judaism and world Jewish peoplehood.

Throughout history Jews have been troubled concerning the purpose and meaning of Jewish existence, but never to so widespread and deep an extent. Moses Maimonides (1135–1204) wrote *The Guide for the Perplexed* for *one* disciple. Today the doubting and perplexed Jews number in the tens of thousands; and it would take more than a Maimonides to allay their misgivings. He had only to address himself to a limited circle of philosophy students; contemporary spiritual leaders have to reckon with the entire Jewish people. They must go beyond the anthropomorphic biblical conception of God to redefine the very meaning of the term. They must motivate Jewish renewal and render its way of life tangible, visible and audible.

How then shall Jews resolve these perplexities? First, they must eliminate the traditional assumptions—supernaturalism and otherworldiness—from Judaism's idea of God, from its concept of Jewish peoplehood and from the traditional way of life. Only a *humanist* worldly perspective can provide relevance, direction and zest to Jewish existence. In the present crisis of life on this planet, the humanist version of Judaism—through promulgation of ethical nationhood—might point the way to the abolition of nuclear war. In the course of its evolving religious civilization the Hebrew prophets proclaimed justice and law as the final determinants of human destiny. They originated and fostered ethical nationhood as religion.

To guide the perplexed of this age the Jewish spiritual leader must demythologize the biblical concept of God and the belief in miracles. He must adapt the Torah with its supernatural world outlook to the indispensable needs of the contemporary world situation. By dispersing the mythical nimbus that enshrouds the Jewish tradition concerning God, miracles, revelation and ritual practices, he will reveal those values which can enhance life.

Although many traditional beliefs cannot be verified, they

served pragmatically to sustain the Jewish people in the face of adversity and attempted annihilation. Demythologizing, rather than discarding such unverifiable assumptions, can help maintain their essential validity. The biblical tradition calls not for the will to believe but for constant seeking and testing of the reality of God. Thus the prophet: "Seek God where He can be found, call upon Him where He is near" (Isa. 55:6); and the Psalmist: "Try and see that the Eternal is good" (Ps. 34:9).

The supernaturalist version of the threefold Jewish tradition interprets God as a being outside and above nature, designates Israel as the nation chosen by God to be an example of virtue and blessedness to other nations, and conceives the Torah as having been dictated by God to Moses for transmission to Israel.

When Jewish history and religion are transposed into the key of humanism, God is conceived as the functioning in nature of the eternally creative process, which, by bringing order out of chaos and good out of evil, actuates man to self-fulfillment. Ancient Israel experienced nature's God as that creative process. It was admonished to follow "God's way of justice and law" (Gen. 18:19). Modern Israel—whose establishment as an independent and viable state strikes the key of naturalism rather than the supernatural motif of divine intervention—should exemplify ethical nationhood. For all Jews—whether citizens of Israel or of other democratic nations—the Torah should provide inspiration and guidance in consonance with "God's way of justice through law."

Ancient Israel's covenant relation to God should be understood in humanist terms as committing the entire Jewish people to ethical nationhood. Just as in the ancient polytheistic world the Israelite nation dedicated itself to the promulgation of ethical monotheism, so in the modern world the Jewish people must undertake the mission of ethical nationhood as a means to international cooperation. Thus might Judaism help avert the nemesis which threatens to overtake mankind.

The Hebrew Bible emphasizes knowledge and wisdom rather than faith as the means for experiencing the reality of God.

"In all thy ways *know* Him," exhorts Proverbs (3:6). But ideology, even if based on a humanist interpretation of the Jewish spiritual heritage, is not enough; it must be translated into a program of action. The old image of the Jew derives from a nation in exile; the new image must project the Jews as a transnational people in dispersion. The unifying factor of a nation is political; the unifying factor of a people is religio-cultural.

World Jewry should be formally reconstructed as a people *de jure*, with a constitution which would set forth the duties and responsibilities of its adherents. That constitution should provide for unity without cultic uniformity or theological dogmatism. The resultant new image of the Jews as a people would counteract the sense of alienation experienced by Jewish youth on nearly every college campus. The crisis in Jewish life stems largely from the centripetal pull of majority populations and their cultures. Unless formal, collective action be taken to regain the cultural and spiritual solidarity of world Jewry, Judaism may not outlast the next three or four generations.

Modern Zionism has demonstrated the Jewish collective will-to-live. But Israel alone cannot save Judaism. The formal re-constitution of the world Jewish people as an organic, self-governing society would strengthen spiritual communion. Were spiritual solidarity to co-exist with religious pluralism it would mitigate the divisive forces of Jewish denominationalism, which, under democracy, is inevitable.

The proposed constitution should close the gap between the Jewish communities in the State of Israel and in the diaspora. It should establish in the diaspora regional Jewish communities that would foster the solidarity of world Jewry. It should spell out the role of the State of Israel as a response not only to the Zionist movement, but to the needs of the entire Jewish people. Witness the migration of Jews from all over the world to settle in, or make pilgrimages to, Israel and their increasing involvement in exchanges on every level—economic, cultural and religious. Jewish citizens of democratic countries must learn to live in two civilizations. By relating the values and resources of their own religious civilization to the problems that beset secular society, Jews may promote the commitment of those countries to ethical nationhood.

Writing in *Conservative Judaism* (Autumn 1967), Elie Wiesel laments: "The trauma of the Holocaust should have produced some change in Jewish life—new books should be written in a different way; a new theology should be created; a new image of Jew and man should be sought for." Is Wiesel calling for a *reconstructionist* program? If his "new image of Jew and man" encompasses both Jewish spiritual solidarity and freedom in matters of belief and cult, then, indeed, Reconstructionism answers his appeal.

The Reconstructionist movement—in its concept of Judaism as an evolving religious civilization—has published at least two dozen volumes on Judaism, a *New Haggadah* and a new liturgical literature—all written in a distinctly "different way" from other books on Judaism. The motto of *The Jewish Reconstructionist*, carried in its first issue (January 11, 1935) and currently, proclaims that the magazine is "dedicated to the advancement of Judaism as a religious civilization, to the up-building of Eretz Israel as the spiritual center of the Jewish People, to the furtherance of universal freedom, justice and peace." It quoted an editorial from the *SAJ Review* (January 20, 1928):

> A solution to the problem of Jewish life depends upon our finding a positive ideology which will enable both Orthodox and Reform, both believers and unbelievers, to meet in common and to work together. It is only by conceiving Judaism as a civilization and not as a general religious movement embracing many sects, that we will be able to construct such an ideology and *reconstruct* the Jewish civilization.

In such books as *The Meaning of God in Modern Jewish Religion* and *Judaism Without Supernaturalism*, this author has expounded a new theology which confronts the main challenge of the Holocaust, the problem of evil. The new theology proposes that instead of dealing with the activity of God in His relation to man, or with what man means to God, it deals rather with the activity of man in his relation to God, or with what God means to man. This is religious humanism. It takes exception to the passage in Isaiah (45:7) which states that God "creates evil." It subscribes to the verse in Proverbs which reads: "Man's wickedness perverts his way of life, and he then blames God for the evil consequences " (19:31). Reconstructionist theology distinguishes between nature and nature's God. Instead of apologizing for God, it demands that man combat human and natural evils in the *name* of God. This theology of religious humanism is the modern equivalent of Maimonides' negative theology.

As for the new image of the Jew, whose absence Wiesel deplores, its creation, along with a new theology, has been the purpose of Reconstructionism. The movement has consistently attacked the fiat of the so-called Sanhedrin summoned by Napoleon in 1805. That assembly virtually destroyed the image of the Jew by declaring religion to be the only bond of Jewish unity. With one stroke of the pen it strove to annul the three-thousand-year-old covenant between God and the people of Israel. It denied the mutual involvement of all Jews which had rendered them responsible for one another's material and spiritual well-being. The Reform movement in Judaism twice confirmed that annulment; in 1845 at Braunschweig, Germany, and in 1886 at Pittsburgh, Pennsylvania. However, in 1937 the menace of Hitler and Nazism, the need for a refuge in Palestine, as well as the growing appeal of Zionism influenced the Central Conference of American Rabbis to reaffirm the unity of the Jewish people as basic to Judaism.

For the record it may be stated that the Reconstructionist conception of Judaism as an evolving religious civilization contributed to that impact of Zionism on the Central Conference of American Rabbis. Moreover, the ideas here associated with the term "civilization" stem from the book *Our Social Heritage* by Graham Wallas published by the Yale University Press in 1921. His thesis is that man is a civilization-building animal, a feature made possible by his ability to acquire through learning and to transmit through teaching a social heritage. So dependent has man come to be upon his social heritage that deprived of it he would either perish or merely vegetate. As a result of the changes which that heritage undergoes in the course of generations, it is subject to continuous criticism and improvement. That constitutes its evolution.

In the light of this conception of man as a civilization builder, the ancient people of Israel was the most creative civilization builder among the peoples of mankind. In Judaism the duty of transmitting the social heritage is a first priority. Likewise in Judaism the phenomenon of continuity in change has been manifest to a greater degree than in other civilizations.

With its inception in 1935, Jewish Reconstructionism took the lead in projecting the image of the authentic Jew, whose Judaism is relevant and vital. The restructured and self-disciplined organic communities of world Jewry—all related to the Jewish community in Israel—should radiate as do the spokes of a wheel from the hub which is Zion. Lacking such organic integration, the prevailing image of the Jew is that of an individual in search of his identity ("What am I?"); and Jewry presents the aspect of a dispirited and disbanded people. Like honorably discharged soldiers who parade on Veterans' Day, Jews assemble on their High Holy Days in sentimental (or conventional) remembrance of things past.

The six-day Israeli-Arab war in June 1967 demonstrated the vitality and solidarity of the Jewish people in its response to shock treatment. But can Jews sustain a continuous, normative way of life—not through crises—but through personal and group commitment to ethical nationhood? Only through the effort to establish God's Kingdom on earth can Jews find meaning and purpose in their existence.

Alone among the nations ancient Israel cherished the dream of righteous nationhood as a prerequisite to world peace. Apocalyptic visions permeate her prophecy and psalmody. They describe "The Day of the Lord [when] He will arbitrate among the nations . . . nation will not lift up sword against nation [and] . . . the earth will be full of the knowledge of the Lord as the waters cover the sea." Unfortunately, that dream, recited fulsomely from pulpits by Jews and non-Jews, has served as a tranquilizer for a sick society in its effort to evade confrontation with an ominous "Day of the Lord." The prophet Amos discerned that "day [as one] of darkness and not light, of blackness with no brightness in it" (Amos 5:18, 20).

The most cruelly tormented victim of evil nationhood has been the Jewish people, whose prophets denounced national iniquity as rebellion against God and who, today, would condemn the mad rivalry among the superpowers which threaten to bring on a nuclear Armageddon. They would agree with Harrison Salisbury, who, in a recent analysis of the world situation, concluded: "The problems are of such a magnitude that only international cooperation—and genuine cooperation by bitterly opposing great powers . . . can resolve them" (*The New York Times*, January 8, 1969).

C. P. Snow, in a study of cataclysmic world problems—which he identified as hunger and starvation, the population explosion and global suicide—drew some consolation from what he termed "a piece of rabbinic wisdom" (*The New York Times*, November 13, 1968). Snow then proceeded to quote the words of Hillel, one of the greatest Jewish sages who lived in the century prior to the destruction of the Second Commonwealth.

What solace could bridge two millennia and apply balm to the wounds of contemporary war-torn and annihilation-threatened society? Although we may not know how Snow applied ancient rabbinic wisdom to modern chaos, the Reconstructionist interpretation of Hillel's probing rhetorical questions might supply the answer:

If I am not for myself, who will be for me?

The individual's *freedom* to choose his own values and course of action is basic to the understanding of human nature. Applied to nations—whose functioning Hillel may have intuited from his knowledge of human nature—this exhortation asserts their autonomy and sovereignty—subject, however, to the limitations of the second proposition:

And being only for myself, what am I?

In making their free choices, individuals and nations must evince a sense of responsibility toward others whose freedom and autonomy demand recognition and respect. Therefore individuals must impose limits upon their own freedom; and nations must accept regulation and modification of absolute sovereignty.

And if not now—when?

These eternal verities must be translated into prompt *action*. Only the freedom and responsibility of upright men can supply the bricks and mortar of ethical nations. Ethical nationhood is now the only basis for the establishment of world order and international peace.

The Reconstructionist version of Judaism as an evolving religious civilization initiated a Copernican revolution in the interpretation of the Jewish spiritual heritage. Rejecting the assumption that the Jewish people must be maintained in order that their religion may live, Reconstructionism declares: *The Jewish religion must be maintained in order that the Jewish people may live.* Hence Reconstructionism bases its modern world outlook upon religious humanism and historical perspective. With this approach the movement has undertaken to demythologize supernatural beliefs and to elucidate many sacrosanct concepts, not in literal terms, but with reference to their spiritual function.

The change from the ancient to the modern universe of discourse calls for unambiguous definitions of current ethical and spiritual concepts as well as for redefinitions of biblical religious concepts. That is a prerequisite for the understanding of the Jewish religion in the new key. Hence the following definitions:

Ideology, perspective or conceptual framework is a series of interrelated ideas about values or non-physical realities which function as factors in human life.

Civilization exists as civilizations. A civilization is the lifestyle of an organic society like a nation or a self-conscious people that is self-perpetuating and self-governing by means of a spiritual heritage which is transmitted from generation to generation and which responds to changing conditions and ever-increasing needs of human existence.

Wisdom, as a sense of values in their normative hierarchy, is that response to all human needs, the satisfaction of which leads to personal self-fulfillment and to international peace.

Human needs may be divided into three categories: biological, psycho-social and spiritual. Spiritual needs are the drives to control the efforts to satisfy the two other categories of needs in order to withstand lust and greed, and to direct those efforts toward the achievement of the goals of wisdom.

Freedom, responsibility and action are elicited from the individual through his involvement in a self-perpetuating and self-governing society, and from each such group through ultimate involvement in the destiny of mankind.

Demythologizing the Hebrew Bible transposes its theology from the key of supernaturalism and what man means to God into the key of religious humanism and what God means to man.

The Jewish people is at present a *de facto* people in need of becoming a *de jure* world, religio-cultural, organic community, with the Land of Israel as its common homeland and with a common history and spiritual heritage.

The Torah is the spiritual heritage of the Jewish people.

Spiritual, holy and ethical are terms for those values which control and direct persons and groups to *want* all that they need to sustain and improve life, but *nothing more* than what they need.

God has been conceived differently in each of the three main stages of Judaism. During the biblical stage God was conceived as Creator, Redeemer and Lawgiver. Ever since then and until modern times God was conceived mainly as the Power that makes for other-worldly salvation. Nowadays God has come to be conceived as that Power in nature and in man which makes for man's this-worldly salvation.

Salvation, like the idea of God, has undergone evolution in the way it was conceived: (1) In Bible times it was conceived as deliverance from this-worldly evils, like slavery, defeat in war, persecution at the hands of enemies or sickness. (2) In pre-modern times since then, salvation meant deliverance from death which is followed by bliss in the hereafter. (3) For those Jews to whom Zionism has meant laboring to upbuild the Land of

Israel and defending it against attack, salvation spells *hagshamah atzmit* (self-realization). For the rest of Jewry, who look to salvation in this world, it means contributing to the creative survival of the Jewish people.

The word *faith* in the English translations of the word *emunah* in the Bible is incorrect. *Emunah* means faithfulness, or trustworthiness.

Judaism, as the evolving religious civilization of the Jewish people, has pioneered in adumbrating man's potential in achieving that collective religious experience which can motivate men and nations to achieve ethical nationhood.

Ethical nationhood—leading to world peace through international cooperation—is no longer optional, but crucial, for creative human survival.

CHAPTER II

Jewish Religion
as Mature Wisdom

I. GROUP RELIGION AS EXPERIENCE

"Nothing within the cognizance of human minds," wrote Arnold J. Toynbee, "is so enigmatic as human nature itself, and the systematic study of it is still in its infancy though it was started more than 2500 years ago in India and the Greek world simultaneously" (*Change and Habit*, p. 12). Inadequate knowledge of human nature underlies the misunderstanding of the role of religion in human life. Most of the works on the psychology of religion fail to differentiate between personal experience—mystical and unsharable, of the kind treated in William James' *Varieties of Religious Experience*—and group religion, the unique manifestation of collective self-consciousness as shared by members of an organic, self-perpetuating and self-governing community. Experience, rather than faith, whose apologists, when challenged, take refuge in a metaphysical "leap of faith," characterizes *normative* group religion.

Some Christian theologians identify faith with the mystic attitude of mind recommended by the Apostle Paul (Rom. 1). For them it consists of the individual's identification with the assumed ever-living presence of Jesus as Son of God. Others define faith as the unquestioning acceptance of the authority of the Church in all matters of doctrine and practice. Traditional

Jewish faith is spelled out in the thirteen principles formulated by Maimonides.

Faith "as a firm conviction of the truth of what is declared by another by way either of testimony or authority without other evidence" has played a role in Judaism ever since the latter half of the Second Commonwealth era, when the Pharisees promulgated the belief in the world to come. Faith thus refers directly to other-worldly salvation as the ultimate destiny of man and only indirectly to God as the Power that makes for salvation. In the Hebrew Bible, however, that kind of faith is as unknown as is the belief in the world to come. The word *emunah* in the Bible means faithfulness or trustworthiness and pertains for the most part to God (cf. Deut. 32:4 and numerous passages in Psalms). When the Israelites beheld the dividing of the waters of the Red Sea so that they might cross it dry-shod, they are said, according to the Christian version, to have "believed in the Lord and in His servant Moses (Exod. 14:31); or according to the Jewish version, to have "had faith in the Lord." Neither version is correct. A more accurate rendition is that of the American translation: "they trusted the Lord and His servant Moses."

The prophet Isaiah expected the Israelites to experience the *importance* to them of God as the ox experiences the importance of its owner and as the ass the importance of its master's crib (Isa. 1:3). The prophet Hosea bewailed the fact that Israel lacked the knowledge of God (Hos. 4:6) in the sense of appreciative experience of what God meant to Israel. The mistranslation of the Hebrew noun *de-ah* and the verb *yada* as referring to knowledge instead of to empirical experience or awareness distorts the biblical notion of man's awareness of God.

In the Hebrew Bible neither the Christian nor the traditional Jewish version of faith figures as the medium of group religious experience. In the eighth century B.C.E., the prophet Amos urged the House of Israel to *seek* God: "Seek me, and you will live" (Amos 5:3). The anonymous prophet of the sixth century B.C.E. called upon his contemporaries to seek God *where* He might be found and to invoke Him *where* He was near (Isa. 55:6). Likewise the Psalmist affirms that "God is near to all who

call Him, who invoke Him in truth" (Ps. 145:18). Indeed, he
advises us to *experience* the reality of God, assuring us that we
will find Him to be good (*ibid.*, 34:8) and therefore appreciate
His importance to us. Moreover, the Deuteronomist, referring
to the state of exile which the Israelites would suffer in retribution for their sins, states: "Yet if *there* you will seek the Lord
your God, you will find Him, provided you seek Him with all
your heart and all your soul" (Deut. 4:29; cf. also Jer. 31:33).
By seeking God the ancients understood learning to appreciate
what God had done for their ancestors. An attitude of trust,
in the sense of *reliance* upon God's promise, is expected as a
consequence of such appreciation of God's importance to man.
Abraham's experience of God's presence is related in Genesis:
"The word of the Lord came to Abram in a vision," assuring
him that his offspring will be as numerous as the stars of heaven.
According to the new translation of the Torah, we read: "And
because he put his *trust* in the Lord he reckoned it to him as
righteousness" (Gen. 15:6).

   *The key to the proper understanding of group religion is the
understanding of the category of wisdom.* Wisdom, as a conceptual tool, assigns to group religion a legitimate place in human
experience. A group religion, as such, is not a matter of reason,
which deals with verifiable fact. Nor is it a matter of intelligence,
which deals with empirical relations of means to ends, although
the more it reckons with reason and intelligence the more
mature it is certain to become. In group religion, *wisdom*, or
the sense of values, functions as a means of enabling human
beings to appreciate why what God does for them is so *important* as to be indispensable. The real problem of religion is
not how to prove the existence of God but how to make sure
that human beings, both individually and collectively, are being
impelled and helped in their efforts to achieve what is most
important to them—salvation or self-fulfillment.

   No word in ancient or modern Hebrew corresponds to the
term "religion." *Dat elohit*, in medieval Hebrew, approximates
that concept as *divine law*. In the Hebrew Bible *hokmah*, which
means wisdom, denotes that which impels man to stand in awe
of God and to obey His laws. Wisdom, as moral and religious

behavior, was common to the ancient civilizations of the Middle East; but only ancient Israel assumed the one and only God to be the source of wisdom as well as of the fulfillment of man's bodily and social needs (cf. Prov. 2:6). In the book of Job we read that God said: "Behold to stand in awe of the Lord, that is wisdom, and to depart from evil, that is foresight" (28:28). From the standpoint of tradition, it is God who reveals wisdom (cf. Prov. 2:6). From the standpoint of reason, it is wisdom that reveals God.

Pre-modern man failed to assign to group religion a legitimate place in *natural* human experience. He assumed that authentic religion must emanate from a *supernatural* source. The rise of science, with the resultant displacement of supernaturalism, influenced Spinoza to supplant religion with ethics. He called his book *Ethics*, not theology, although its subject matter derives from his idea of God. By identifying God with nature or reality and by reducing ethics to a rational or objective discipline analogous to geometry, Spinoza arrived at an *intellectual* "love of God." Thus he concluded that ethics, as wisdom, is the source of man's knowledge of God.

Immanuel Kant assigned religion to the domain of faith as a practical matter and an object of the will rather than of speculative metaphysics. A philosopher in the classic tradition, he maintained that the criterion of authenticity applied only to sensate experience from the point of view of time, space and the logical categories. Hence there was no room for God in his *Critique of Pure Reason*. Certainly from the perspective of reason which deals only with sensate experience, the only valid categories are those of time and space. If as great a thinker as Kant ignored human *needs* in his exposition of pure reason, it was because he lived before the discovery of the category of *value*.

The authentic nature of group religion owes much to the recent discovery of value as a concept-tool. In 1924 this category was expounded at length by F.C.S. Schiller in an article written for *Hastings' Encylopedia of Religion and Ethics:* "*Value* is one of the last of the great philosophic topics to have received recognition . . . Its discovery was probably the greatest philosophic achievement of the 19th century, but opinions on the subject are not yet crystallized, and it is still one of the growing points of philosophy and one which seems likely to overshadow other issues." A value is whatever satisfies a human need. Thus economic, cultural and spiritual needs have each their corresponding values or objects that satisfy them.

Values, though invisible and intangible, are as real as visible and tangible facts or realities. As psychic and social facts or realities, values are far more potent as fact makers or factors, in the sense of producing results. The God concept, properly understood as a factor in ordering the life of men and nations, is the most potent and creative factor in human existence.

As recently as 1952 the *Synopticon of Great Books of the Western World* contained no reference to value. Evidently the faculties of the University of Chicago—whose educationists selected the Great Books—did not recognize value as a valid philosophic category. For them value had only an economic relevance, as though we could speak only of economic progress but not of cultural or spiritual progress.

The *Synopticon* also failed to grasp the significance of the concept *wisdom*. "The phrase 'modern science' needs no elucidation," it adds, "but if anyone were to speak of 'modern wisdom,' he would have to explain its meaning." It goes on to define wisdom in terms of an intellectual rather than an emotionally volitional virtue. That error is rooted in Platonic philosophy, which regarded only the ideas of the intellect as reality in contrast to emotions and volitions which it deemed subjective and transitory. That assumption put off the discovery of value until the latter part of the nineteenth century.

In contrast with the ideationist fallacy, the emotions and the volitions as articulated by the imagination are the *primary* substance of human experience. At first, mentation is the product of imagination which takes the form of mythology. As the human mind evolves, *reason* corrects the imaginary thought process. When the mind first generalizes and articulates its needs, it conceives sources of satisfaction which are imaginary. Thus arise the concepts of spirits, demons, numina and gods which early civilizations reckoned as wisdom. They referred to one or another specific need which the various spirits helped to satisfy, provided the group conformed to a prescribed behavior pattern. The God of ancient Israel, being the one and only authentic God, was conceived *functionally* as meeting *all* human needs in such a way as to impel and help the human species achieve the purpose for which it was intended. To be sure, the proper noun YHWH does imply that God was conceived in substantive terms. However, there are at least forty texts in the Hebrew Bible referring to God as *being* the God of the people of Israel. Hence the biblical idea of God is mainly a functional one; His functions are Creator, Redeemer and Lawgiver.

To place public or group religion in the perspective of mature wisdom, those needs and human values that constitute religious experience must be identified.

Human needs comprise: (1) biological needs for health, security and mating, the satisfaction of which is experienced as well-being; (2) psycho-social needs for appreciation and influence, the satisfaction of which yields a sense of power; and (3) spiritual needs, which constitute the human differentia, and which are the needs for controlling and directing human efforts in satisfying biological needs without indulgence in lust and in satisfying psycho-social needs without surrender to greeds. To satisfy the need for control and direction, the individual requires involvement with his self-governing, self-perpetuating organic community, such as a family, clan, tribe, nation or people.

"The individual man," wrote Roscoe Pound, "the social unit himself, needs the restraint of the inner order of a group or association of some sort in order to keep in balance on the one hand the aggressive instinct of self-assertion and on the other hand the social instinct of cooperation which are deep-seated in each of us" (*Ideological Differences and World Order*, edited by F.S.C. Northrop, p. 1). He also points out that the ethical idea of law was regarded in antiquity as authoritatively formulated morals. In the course of time law came to be regarded as "the most specialized and the most organized form of social control, and of social control as directed to the maintaining, furthering and transmitting of civilization." This fact is substantiated by the pioneering of Judaism from its very inception as nothing less than a civilization, a civilization which is the synthesis of the spiritual with the natural.

Hence, man's spiritual needs can be met only among those who pursue a common way of life, speak the same language and communicate in the same universe of thought and discourse. The common good of the organic group requires that the individual drives of its constituents should not overpower the well-being of others. In his striving for competence or power the individual must be restrained from greed and aggression. Thus every organic community must legislate for its members and enforce sanctions against their violation of law. Through the like-mindedness of its members a group comes to be cohesive, stable and self-disciplined. The group develops a common mind and common will, particularly the will to live, by transmitting its spiritual heritage from generation to generation.

The Maturation of Wisdom

In the ancient Middle East there emerged a normative sense of life's values which stressed the humanization of man. Its concept of *wisdom* differs from reason as value, or the subjective significance of a fact, differs from objective facticity. A fact is descriptive; a value is normative and therefore a factor in being a guide to action. Both are essential functions of the human mind. Without wisdom the reasoning faculty cannot fathom the meaning of God or man; both are correlative terms of value. *God's divinity manifests itself in the fulfillment of the human in man, and man's humanity is realized to the extent that it cooperates with the divinity of God.*

Modern scientific methods have revealed a reality that is often at variance with values which ancient wisdom attached to various experiences. Thus *reason*, which deals with facts, proves certain assumptions of wisdom to be illusory. Wisdom matures when it accepts the dicta of reason. Just as the immature wisdom of the Bible encountered the challenge of Hellenistic philosophy in the writings of Philo and Maimonides, it is now forced to defend its position against Higher Criticism and the scientific study of biblical texts.

In functioning along scientific lines the human mind develops *intelligence,* which is the self-conscious process of relating means to ends. The wisdom of the Bible may be compatible with the rational discoveries of Higher Criticism yet prove irrelevant to contemporary issues of democracy versus communism, of nationalism versus cosmopolitanism and of peace versus war. In this nuclear age, when man possesses the fire power to trigger a universal cataclysm, religion becomes irrelevant if it abstains from a massive effort to avert the doom that threatens the human species.

Since wisdom represents the initial value judgments of the human mind, it throws light on the function of religion. According to the anthropologist Emile Durkheim, all primitive societies engage in collective practices which constitute "elementary forms of religious experience." The failure of many great thinkers to grasp the concept of wisdom has involved them in error with regard to the authentic function of reason. They should have restricted reason to denote the facticity of things and situations rather than extended its applicability to "oughtness," which relates to values. Grotius maintained that reason without revelation and without the help of God could dictate what was right and just. Justice O. W. Holmes, whose reasoning ability was beyond reproach, maintained that whatever the state could enforce was inherently just and right and that such enforcement constituted the ethical aspect of law. Surprisingly enough, there is warrant for this view in Spinoza's *Tractatus Theologico Politicus.* To such absurdities men of extraordinary mental caliber committed themselves because of their failure to distinguish between the functions of wisdom and of reason.

The foregoing discussion of values points to religion, with its ideas about gods or God, as primarily the expression of man's response to his needs. Pagan or polytheistic religions, in their limited wisdom, scarcely recognized differences of degree or a hierarchal order among those needs. Every need—security, health, mating, knowledge, love, cooperation, competence or well-being—was experienced as indispensable and hence as a matter of religious concern. That concern gave rise to myths about gods as objects of worship and to inhibitions in the form of taboos. The satisfaction of needs was accompanied by imaginative experience which elicited emotions of fear or love and which was projected onto the deified object.

The great religions of the West and the Near East establish a kind of hierarchal order among values—an order deriving from the *spiritual need for control and direction in the effort to satisfy the various other needs.* The Far Eastern religions, however, maintain that biological and psycho-social needs evoke evil desires which corrupt human nature and mar human life. They therefore teach that man's salvation consists in suppressing those needs through ascetic self-discipline in order to arrive at the goal of Nirvana—virtually non-being or nothingness. The Buddha is said to have found his consolation in a doctrine and discipline that would eliminate, instead of direct, all desires. Those who renounced asceticism and yielded to their desires were condemned to various transmigrations until they atoned for their guilt and attained the sublime state of Nirvana. Although he deprecated the worship of gods, Buddha, by his teachings and way of life, became indispensable to the attainment of salvation. Inevitably, he himself came to be worshiped as a god.

Any of the classical systems of the East—Vedanta, Yoga, Buddhism, Zen—requires the individual seeker to adopt an austere way of life and often to undergo a long, arduous training period in seclusion. Most of the Orient's great scriptures emphasize the need for giving up worldly pleasures and material possessions and for overcoming desire and attachment to persons. The world per se is of no value, but rather an obstacle to spiritual progress. "Let him . . . acquire freedom from all desires. Nothing that is eternal can be gained by what is not eternal," says Meindaka Upanishad (II, 12). (Frederick Holek and Eleanor Cate, "Ex Oriente Lux," *Christian Century*, March 5, 1969).

Hebraic Versus Hellenic Concepts of Wisdom

The Hebraic and Hellenic civilizations evolved differing types of wisdom or religion. Each attempted to bring order into men's efforts to satisfy their needs for well-being and efficacy.

The Hebrews stressed involvement with the nation as the most effective source of control and satisfaction of human needs. The need for belonging arises naturally from the need to be needed. The Israelite nation exercised such control over the life of its adherents because all were regarded as dependent upon the one God, the Creator of the world, its King and Savior. Ancient Israel, which was a theocracy, ordered its entire life in keeping with the regimen prescribed by priests and prophets who spoke in the name of God. Its regimen of conduct was spelled out in the 613 commandments ascribed to the one God, whose name was YHWH. Those commandments were further defined and elaborated in what came to be known as Torah, both written and oral.

A passage in the Torah, ascribed to Moses, formulates the purpose and meaning of ancient Israel's existence:

> Here am I teaching you, as YHWH my God commanded me, to observe statutes and ordinances in the land you are entering to possess. Be careful, then, that you observe them, for that will prove your wisdom and understanding to the nations; when they hear all these rules they will say, "This great nation is indeed a wise understanding people." For what great nation has a God so near to it, as YHWH our God is whenever we invoke Him? What great nation has rules and regulations as just as all this code that I am putting before you now? [Deut. 4:5-8].

In specific terms God had promised each of the three patriarchal founders of the nation that through their descendants all the families of the earth would invoke blessings on themselves (cf. Gen. 12:3; 26:4, 28:14). The people of Israel would thus serve as a paradigm to the nations of the world.

Those teachings did not pertain to some esoteric philosophy which only a few spiritually gifted men could grasp. They have been built into the collective consciousness of the Jewish people for twenty-five hundred years. No matter how unreflective the individual Jew may have been, he apprehended those teachings. Although seldom aware of all their implications, he thought now and then of mankind as a whole and in terms of justice as emanating from the very nature of the universe whose Creator, Maintainer and Ruler was the one and only authentic God. That awareness accounts for the overriding role of religion in the pre-modern history of the Jewish people and for the impact of its religious civilization on the Christian and Moslem civilizations.

A radically different way of reckoning with man's *ultimate* needs emerged in the Hellenic world. By the fifth century B.C.E., individual thinkers known as Sophists questioned the divine origin of the basic laws by which the city states of Ionia and Greece were governed. They sought in the conception of justice a rationally acceptable basis for those laws. Socrates declared that justice was not merely a subjective value whose application depended upon the arbitrary will of the ruling clique. As Plato expounded Socrates' teaching, the problem of justice in the conduct of a state was analogous to the problem which the human individual faced in harmonizing the three aspects of his nature: the intellectual, the emotional and the practical. Thus Hellenic wisdom (*sophia*) came to be identified with *reflection*, which alone made life worth living, instead of with *wisdom* which, according to the Hebrews, meant obedience to the will of God (cf. Job 28:28).

The Hebraic and the Hellenic concepts of life and value are in marked contrast. For the Hebrews it was paramount to belong to a nation to which God, who had created the world, revealed a way of life. "Justice through law" would enable every member of the nation to achieve fulfillment or salvation (cf. Gen. 18–19). Such a nation believed itself and all living creatures to be governed by the laws of the one world Ruler who kept the stars in their courses. The Greek philosophers maintained that only those, who through speculative thought arrived at a knowledge of ultimate reality, could build a state. Hence only a class society ruled by philosopher-kings could dispense justice to the *hoi polloi* and help them fulfill their needs to the advantage of all concerned.

In the Bible, the wisdom by which man is expected to control and direct his life reflects the wisdom by which God's laws govern all nature:

> It is He who made the earth by His power,
> Who established the world by His wisdom,
> And stretched out the heavens by His understanding.
> When He thunders, there is a storm of waters in the heavens,
> And He causes vapors to rise from the ends of the earth;
> He makes the lightnings for the rain,
> And brings out the wind from His storehouse,
> But men are stupid and senseless [Jer. 10:12–14].

> Even the stork in the heavens knows her seasons
> The turtle dove, swallow and crane know of their coming
> But my people know not the ordinance of the Lord [Jer. 8:7].

Both Hebraic wisdom and Hellenic philosophy, in charting a course for man to achieve his full humanity, established a *scale* of values. Although the two civilizations differed in their conceptions of Godhood, its value was preeminent. In the Hebraic view, Godhood implied being the Creator of mankind as well as its King and Provider. The Hellenes interpreted Godhood as the Active Intellect that ordered all of nature and enabled the philosopher-kings to establish and govern states. Both the Hebrew religion and Hellenic philosophy mythologized their respective ideas of Godhood. Hebrews and Greeks hypostasized their respective insights in order to discern in the natural world responsiveness to man's need for self-fulfillment or salvation.

When one of Plato's disciples tried to establish a state on the island of Syracuse along the lines formulated in *The Republic*, he was assassinated by a fellow disciple. This put an end to that kind of experiment. To a certain extent the Catholic Church tried to follow the Platonic model. Their vicars in Christ received ordination from Christ's Apostles and their papal successors, who invested them with authority to rule over a world empire. Although Catholic power has been eroded by the political power of nations and the religious challenges of various Protestantisms, it succeeded in controlling an extensive and disciplined spiritual realm. The Hebraic method of dealing with man's needs and their satisfaction welded nomadic tribes into one nation whose religious monotheism is a prerequisite to ethical nationhood.

As long as the human mind found supernaturalism congenial to its world outlook, traditional religion demonstrated its validity. It enabled the Jewish people to survive and fulfill its purpose by testifying to the greatness of God (cf. Isa. 43:21). Can the Jewish people survive without the aura and authority of revelation? The mere momentum of tradition or social heritage cannot energize the collective will to live. That impulse must be motivated by a rational and relevant conception of God which deals with matters of man's ultimate concern. The survival of the human species is at stake. As a result of his unlimited power of destruction man must exercise all his spiritual powers to master the forces of aggression in his own nature. *Nations, in their collective capacity and in their relations to one another, must control their political, economic, social and cultural activities with the aim of fostering ethical nationhood and international peace.*

That consummation is not a matter of prudence. It is a manifestation of the cosmic syndrome which includes the physical, biological and psycho-social processes. That consummation indicates a Power in the cosmos which fosters the creative survival of the human species. In its dimension of Godhood it endows the self-perpetuating, self-disciplining Jewish community with purpose and meaning. But that Godhood must be demythologized and reinterpreted as humanist theology if the Jewish people is to renew itself and survive creatively.

In the Graeco-Roman world the role of the Stoics is illuminating. They established neither a group religion nor an organic community capable of self-control and self-direction. By mini-mizing the individual's needs and their satisfaction, they in-fluenced some of the Roman elite to adopt asceticism as a way of life. Although the Stoics contributed to the codification of Roman law, they had no moral effect on the *collective* con-sciousness of the Roman Empire. The Roman people never developed a collective sense of guilt. The *Aeneid*, which Virgil wrote to inculcate a collective Roman consciousness, never achieved that purpose.

The God of the Hebrews is manifest in their collective self-awareness. The significance of the proper noun YHWH for God is conveyed later by the abstract term *Shekinah*, or *Presence*. "Wherever Jews went into exile, the *Shekinah* was with them" (*Megillah* 29a). The concept of justice through law, which constitutes "God's way" (Gen. 18:19), is intended for the nation in both its domestic and foreign affairs. The God of Abraham, Isaac and Jacob created the Hebrew nation to be an example to other nations and to testify to His sovereignty over mankind. Every nation in the world should experience His driving mankind toward international amity and abide by "His way of justice through law." Traditional Jewish liturgy for the High Holidays stresses God's sovereignty as destined to unite all the nations of the world who, in accepting His dominion, are expected to limit their sovereignty.

The Religion of Man and the Blasphemy of Superman

The most striking validation of Hebrew wisdom has taken place during the last hundred years. Never has that religion been so brazenly challenged, nor with such tragic consequences. During the late nineteenth century Friedrich Nietzsche tried to subvert the values of the Judeo-Christian tradition. Steeped in classic philosophy, which did not regard involvement in organic community as a prerequisite to individual self-fulfillment, he arrived at the bizarre and brutal notions set forth in the *Transvaluation of Values*. Dazzled by the Darwinian discovery of the evolutionary process in nature, Nietzsche applied the principle of natural selection for survival—mainly the strongest or the most cunning—to mankind. That discovery had the impact of a revelation. He rejected the basic teachings of traditional religion and morality with their compassion for the weak and the oppressed. He denounced such life values on the ground that they would lead to the deterioration of the human species and advocated the *will-to-power*, with the aim of evolving the superman.

This iconoclastic philosophy struck a responsive chord in the Germanic mind at a time when it was attuned to nationalist ambitions and romantic race theories which idealized the Aryan race and denigrated others. Out of the witches' brew of Nietzscheanism and Aryan nationalism emerged Fascism and Nazism, which almost succeeded in replacing civilization with a highly systemized and brutal barbarism. Such demonic madness had been denounced by the prophet Isaiah, who described some of his contemporaries as "those who call good evil and evil good, who count darkness as light and light as darkness, who count bitter as sweet and sweet as bitter. Woe to those who think themselves wise and clever" (Isa. 5:20–21).

The vicious folly of the Nietzschean philosophy—with its assumptions about the human species, its elimination of the unfit and its cultivation of a race of supermen through the unbridled will-to-power—has sown the dragon's teeth of several European and of two world wars. Today such nihilist notions could bring mankind to the brink of annihilation through total war. To avert the cataclysm, mankind must fall back on the old wisdom of Hebraic religion and morality: *the need to make individuals and nations fit to survive.* Through involvement with and commitment to organic communities, their constituents will be rendered fit to live and develop their full potential.

The Prophetic Call for Total Involvement

From its inception biblical religion has called upon every individual and organic community to seek involvement in an organic communal unit—the individual in an organic group and the group in a federation of organic groups. Such is the

Kingdom of God which the Hebrew prophets envisioned for the Household of Israel. Next in moral and spiritual stature to the prophet Moses, who laid the foundation of the Household of Israel, was the prophet Jeremiah, who articulated its international role. The very reluctance with which, like Moses, he accepted the role as "a prophet to the nations" to exercise his "authority over nations and kingdoms, to tear, to break down, to shatter, to pull down, to build up, and to plant" (Jer. 1:5, 10) testifies to the transcendent Power that impels *mankind* toward creative survival.

What are those traits that make for international involvement and commitment? They stem from a sense of mutual responsibility toward the human community, beginning with the family and terminating, at present, with the nation. The Israelite nation alone through its spokesmen, the prophets, conceived of mutual responsibility as extending beyond the nation to which one belonged. They envisaged all nations as learning to experience a sense of reciprocal responsibility.

Reciprocal responsibility, which finds expression in various ethical traits, is the *sine qua non* for the stability and welfare of human society. Justice spelled out into law—which prohibits doing unto others what one would not have others do to one's self—and loyalty—which demands that man reckon with his fellow men and fellow nations as ends in themselves and not only as means—are indispensable to organic, self-perpetuating and self-governing communities. Just as the essence of wisdom in the Bible is responsibility, the essence of folly is irresponsibility. The Bible characterizes the wicked person as a godless irresponsible fool (cf. Ps. 14 and 53).

The fantastic notion that organic and self-governing communities came into being as the result of deliberate social contract has been rejected. Human communities, like subhuman ones, are the product of natural forces that operate in the cosmos in the form of physical and biological laws. The theory of reciprocal responsibility is the conscious human manifestation of the principle whereby everything in nature is both cause and effect of everything else. It corresponds with the universal law of polarity whereby everything in the universe, from the minutest electron to the vastest star, is both self-active and interactive, independent and interdependent.

2. DEMYTHOLOGIZING WHAT MAN MEANS TO GOD

It has become urgent to analyze the mythological elements of the Jewish religious tradition and to identify those aspirations or spiritual values in it which are relevant for individual fulfillment and universal peace. The functional, rather than allegorical, method of demythologizing the Torah should reveal the purpose and meaning of Jewish existence. When Philo likened the four rivers in the Garden of Eden to the four virtues of man, he wrote in the idiom of allegory. But the function of the Garden of Eden story can be discerned only after it is stripped of myth and allegory to uncover its essence in terms of moral and spiritual values. To demythologize the story of the Garden of Eden therefore means to get at the pattern of human life and the universal spiritual values which are relevant even though they do not represent literal fact.

In transposing the mythical theology of the Torah into the key of modern humanist theology, the functional method of interpretation will be applied to the following subjects: the introductory myths of the Torah; the Decalogue as the revelation of the Divine in man; and the meaning of God in history.

The Introductory Myths of the Torah

The myth of Creation in the entire first chapter of Genesis is a figment of the primitive imagination. The story about the Flood depicts a heaven with windows through which the waters poured down to swell the waters below the earth.

The myth that God made man in His own image implies that God and man share the transcendent element of Godhood. Thus man only attains humanity when his life reflects the reality of God. Though man and beast have much in common, the divine in man sets him radically apart. Unlike other great civilizations of the Near East which worshiped animals as gods, the world of the Bible distinguished between the human and the subhuman. This humanistic and moral idea defines the function of the mythical Creation story.

Ostensibly, the Garden of Eden myth conveys God's expectations of man; God did not want man to eat the fruit of the tree of knowledge of good and evil. But what is meant by "the knowledge of good and evil?" When that phrase occurs in Deuteronomy 1:39, it reads: "your children that this day have no knowledge of good or evil." And young King Solomon asked God to give him "an understanding heart to judge Thy people, that I may discern between good and evil" (I Kings 3:9). These passages declare that the knowledge of good and evil relates to the difference between right and wrong and that God, not man, is the sole source of such knowledge. (The Hebrew Bible did not propound moral relativism or situational ethics.)

Transposed into humanist terms, the Garden of Eden legend emphasizes that man's self-interest is no gauge of right and wrong. Only a transcendent awareness of reciprocal responsibility in accord with the dictates of nature's God can determine moral and spiritual values. When Cain killed Abel and subsequently disavowed all responsibility for his brother, he took the law unto himself and set into motion the degeneration of the human species. Violence resulted from Adam's transgression in substituting self-will for the law and order which are the will of God.

As man's transgressions multiplied, the contagion corrupted all creation. Therefore, the myth relates, God regretted that He had created man and brought on the Flood. But in the exceptional character of Noah—who is portrayed as reflecting the divine purpose—God discerned the creativity that overcomes the entropy in nature and in man. After the Flood, which virtually returned creation to chaos, God dictated to Noah the law and order which, if observed, would assure the survival of mankind. The myth represents God as promising no more floods or cataclysms. Ironically, it is man who now has the power to turn the earth back to original chaos. A functional interpretation of the Flood myth and of God's covenant should warn mankind to bring its morality into the same century as its weaponry.

In a naive attempt to explain the origin of nations, the author of the City and Tower of Babel myth portrayed God as confounding the language of mankind. Through division men would be prevented from contravening the divine purpose of creation: "And the Lord said: 'Behold they are one people, and they all have one language; and this is only what they begin to do; and now nothing will be withholden from them, which they propose to do'" (Gen. 11:6). But the evils of nationhood are not inherent in the division of mankind into ethnic groups and national entities. It is the ethical character of nationhood which decides whether division and diversity bode good or ill for creative survival. Without ethical motivation in this age of megathon missiles and "acceptable" ninety (as opposed to one hundred and twenty) million casualties, the menacing reality forecast in the myth may come to pass: "Behold [the nations] have one language [that is the capability of annihilation]; and now nothing will be withholden from them, which they propose to do."

When Abraham welcomed God and His two angels, disguised as strangers, their colloquy sounds the keynote of the religion of Israel. Mythically, the episode relates how YHWH instructed Abraham in what was to be the distinctive moral trait of the nation to be founded by him. That nation was to set an example to the other nations of the way to administer justice through law. Hence the display of the legal process as later set forth in the Torah, including the testimony of at least two witnesses (Deut. 17:6). Without such testimony even the flagrant violence of Sodom and Gomorrah against strangers could not be punished. Discounting the element of myth in this legend, we have here unmistakable evidence of ancient Israel's aspiration to function as a paradigm of ethical nationhood.

When Abraham received a last-minute reprieve from the divine command to sacrifice his only son, Isaac, the angel of the Lord said: "Do not lay hands on the lad . . . for I know now that you revere God." Why does this myth stress reverence for God? Because Abraham, by his unquestioning obedience to

God's will, made possible the rise of an eternal people. He renounced the cycle of violence and lawlessness which Adam and Eve, through their disobedience, had precipitated.

However, the fact that so bizarre a myth could find a place in the Torah does call for an explanation. That story undoubtedly arose at a time when human sacrifice was practiced in some of the pagan nations with which ancient Israel came in contact. Those who first learned to worship the God YHWH no doubt refused to be outdone by the pagans in their devotion to YHWH, to whom human sacrifice was an abomination. Thus out of the tension between those two conflicting attitudes toward YHWH there was bound to arise the kind of a myth in which that conflict was resolved. Abraham was tested and he withstood the test.

The Bible defines the goal of Jewish existence in terms of the glorification of God. In Deutero-Isaiah God refers to ancient Israel as "My people, Mine elect, the people which I formed for Myself that they might tell of My praise" (Isa. 43:20–21). How seriously Israel regarded the glorifying of God is manifest in its unique genius for psalmody. To be sure, polytheistic religions have psalmody. But praising the gods singly or in concert—in the hope of winning their favor or deflecting their wrath—has nothing in common with the Hebraic conception. The frequent reference in the Bible to the special significance of knowing God's name seems almost certainly to prove that the term "name" in Hebrew either denotes or at least connotes the idea of function. Thus we read: "I will set him on high because he knows my name; when he calls upon me I will answer him" (Ps. 91:14–15).

Even in this mythical form the notion that God created man to honor Him presupposes a radical and qualitative difference between the human and subhuman. Ancient Israel refused to deify animals because of their superior physical powers. So profound was its abhorrence of such blasphemy that the Israelites were enjoined from representing the Deity in any form.

The biblical conception of God is unique. Great thinkers such as Kepler and Spinoza conceived of God as synonymous with nature. To the biblical scholar Ezekiel Kaufman, the God of Israel represented purposiveness in antithesis to blind fate. Insofar as nature is creative and functions according to the will of God, predictable law may be identified with that creative aspect of nature which impels and helps man to achieve creative survival. Despite its mythical aspects, the traditional belief that God created man to glorify Him had all the force of objective fact. That concept impelled ancient Israel to accept the praise of God as its mission in life and the *raison d'être* for its nationhood. It became the chief motivation for Jewish survival in the midst of hatred and persecution. Its authentic elements of individual and collective commitment still define the goal and purpose of Jewish survival.

Midway in the third century before the common era, Judaism —influenced by Zoroastrian civilization—adopted the belief in the world to come (*olam ha-ba*). Drawing cold comfort from the biblical doctrine of retributive justice and the undeserved suffering of the righteous, post-exilic Jews embraced the myth of the hereafter where the inequities of this world would be righted. According to Rabbinic tradition, which went into specifics, some virtues and pieties earn interest in this world, with the capital reserved for the world to come. Equal in merit to all those virtues and pieties is the study of Torah (*Misnah, Peah*, I). When the study of Torah was lauded as the surest means of earning a portion in the world to come, this notion transformed the entire style of Jewish life.

In the modern scientific world the myth of reward and punishment in the next world has lost all credibility. Nor does man repose much confidence in earthly justice (retributive or benign) at the hand of a supernatural Being to whom he may still address formal prayers. Nevertheless, these myths embody profound spiritual and psychological insights which throw light upon the anxieties and intuitive strivings of mankind. If the desire for a higher order of existence motivates man to undertake his own creative metamorphosis, the myth of bliss in the hereafter may come closer to realization on earth.

Myths express the creative genius of a people. But they must be recognized as pointers to deep underlying values and aspirations. Judaism is enriched by the validity, not by the facticity, of its mythical heritage. This notion should liberate many modern Jews and especially college-bred youth, from the burden of professing untenable and irrelevant beliefs. Demythologizing that heritage should help overcome the alienation and apathy experienced by many who have been "living in two worlds: one dead, the other powerless to be born."

The Decalogue as the Revelation of the Divine in Man

The Decalogue defines the "way which God was represented as having revealed to Abraham for the instruction of his progeny" (Gen. 18:19). Seven of the Ten Commandments are prohibitions—a circumstance too often stressed in derogation of their moral value. In his book *Living Philosophies*, James Thurslow Adams countered that specious argument:

> A good many impulsive and expansive natures object to moral codes on the score that they are repressive, that they consist of "Thou shalt nots." There are two comments to be made on this objection. The first is that negative commands in general are far less limiting than positive ones . . . Consider the much abused Ten Commandments of the Jews. Is there not a much larger sphere of free action left us by Thou shalt not steal, or commit adultery, or bear false witness than by the command Thou shalt love thy neighbor as thyself? . . . On the other hand, if self-expression is good, it also becomes evident to what we may call "the subconscious wisdom of the race" that it must have limits, or it ceases to be good, both for the individual himself and for society . . . It becomes clear that, if we are to get the good out of self-expression, we must introduce somewhere the negations of self-restraint [pp. 165–166].

Each of the Ten Commandments is concerned with ethical behavior from the standpoint of humanist theology. The three positive commands direct man toward justice; the seven negative behests prohibit his surrender to the evil forces of idolatry, violence and licentiousness.

1. *I, YHWH, am your god*—The First Commandment is

addressed to the nation as a whole, as well as to every individual. Divinity is manifest as justice in action, in the historic event of Israel's redemption from Egypt.

2. *You shall have no other gods beside Me*—Monotheism implies a universe whose cosmic polarity of independence and interdependence fosters the fulfillment or salvation of individuals and nations. Individual needs are regarded as a totality, comprising biological, social and spiritual needs, with the spiritual controlling and directing the satisfaction of the biological and psycho-social needs. Since polytheism had no conception of organic interrelatedness, each need was provided for by a particular deity. Often both gods and men were in conflict, with the result that human beings and nations had to propitiate offended gods and pit one against another. The normal attitude of the Jew toward God is one of imitating His "way of justice through law."

So much for the theological relevance of the Second Commandment. Psychologically, it exposes the godlessness of affluent civilizations and "great societies." Since a god represents that which a human being *values* as indispensable, a wrong sense of values is as irreligious as the worship of false gods.

3. *You shall not swear falsely by the name of YHWH your God*—The name of God, "the Power that makes for righteousness," must not be invoked to justify self-serving conduct on the part of individuals and groups. The justification of unworthy means to ends, even if the latter are considered worthy, is a form of taking God's name in vain.

4. *Remember the Sabbath day and keep it holy*—The godly life is one in which the *totality* of human nature is fulfilled. The Sabbath affords man leisure for meditation and detachment from mundane pursuits. It heightens his consciousness of life's spiritual values.

5. *Honor your father and your mother*—The family is the basic unit wherein the human differentia of the child begins to emerge. The Talmud describes parents as partners with God in the life of the person (*Kiddushin* 30b). If the child's education and the parents' convictions share in the same universe of thought, the child will probably accept the values of his

parents—which is the essence of his honoring them. If, however, the child's general education belongs to a different and generally accepted universe of thought and discourse from that of the parents, they should reeducate themselves and learn how to reinterpret their inherited spiritual values in those of the child so as to give him reason for honoring them. Otherwise, there is bound to be an unbridgeable gap between parents and children.

6. *You shall not murder*—The original prohibition of individual murder should be extended to include any form of irresponsible behavior which threatens human existence. The time must come, and that very soon, when aggressive war will have to be outlawed as wholesale murder.

7. *You shall not commit adultery*—The sexual urge in human beings should seek fulfillment in keeping with the ethical principle formulated by Kant: "So act as to treat humanity both in your own person and in that of any other person, always as an end also, never as a means only." As long as child-rearing is family-based, this commandment is vital. Preservation of the family in which children can be reared to responsible adulthood should be a top priority of civilization. According to Karl Jaspers:

> Any man can take marriage and the family seriously, finding therein faithfulness, responsibility, understanding, the joy of mutuality in living, the security of origin, and the source of justice—all in spite of the statistics about the decline of the family and the description of its desolation. If the Kinsey report reveals that 75 per cent of the men want extramarital sexual intercourse and 50 per cent actually practice it, these statistics are neither the expression of what should be, nor a determination of what is "natural" for man [*Religion and Culture*, edited by Walter Leibrecht, p. 42].

8. *You shall not steal*—Without honesty in human relations no organic society can function. Dishonesty in any form is theft; it deprives the victim not only of his property, but often of his right to know the truth. In biblical Hebrew "to steal one's heart" is to mislead or outwit (Gen. 31:20).

9. *You shall not bear false witness*—Thanks to mass communications media, to say nothing of the "Gutenberg galaxy," there

are more opportunities for spreading slander than were ever dreamed of in biblical lexicons.

Jews have been libeled and victimized through the centuries by the Stoic Apion of Alexandria, against whom Josephus wrote his *Contra Apion,* and by the charge of deicide in the Gospels and by the Fathers of the Church. During the Middle Ages the Jews were accused of bringing the Black Plague to Europe by poisoning the wells. The medieval blood accusation against Jews was revived as recently as 1844 in Damascus, and in Czarist Russia where it incited the perpetrators of the Kishinev pogrom in 1905. Even in democratic America, Henry Ford reprinted and circulated the forgery known as *The Protocols of the Elders of Zion,* and Father Coughlin broadcast his slanders against the Jews from his church-based radio.

The Decalogue sets forth the goals to be achieved through the education of the conscience. Although belief in their divine revelation no longer motivates man to unquestioning obedience, the Ten Commandments are no less authentic. They derive their authority—not from an outworn belief in God as a Personal Being—but from an authentic comprehension of human nature as a syndrome of life, mind and spirit. Rooted in the past these new forms of thought about God and man will bear fruit in the intellectual climate of the present.

The Meaning of God in History

Through the mythological interpretation of human experience ancient civilizations personified the impersonal and reified the abstract. Hence the biblical universe of discourse is largely mythological and its conception of God is anthropomorphic. Does the recognition of this fact denigrate the Bible's credibility or its value as a guide for our day? Far from it! The Bible could never have played the leading role in the humanization of man if it had not dealt with basic and universal human needs. As wisdom matures through experience and knowledge, correct procedures to satisfy those needs should supersede the secondary ones.

From its inception Hebraic monotheism was based upon

authentic wisdom. What was affirmed as an apodictic assumption in the Hebrew Bible concerning human needs may be regarded as the first philosophy of history. So persistent are the problems of human life dealt with in the Bible, so comprehensive and consistent is the scope of its philosophy of history, that despite the naiveté of some of its concepts the Bible is vitally relevant today for the renewal not only of the Jewish people but of all mankind.

The biblical philosophy of history is cast in the form of a drama, with God and Israel in the foreground as the principal protagonists. Against the backdrop of other nations Israel is presented as their paradigm. As the drama unfolds, it emphasizes that *human beings can learn to control and direct the satisfaction of their vital needs only when they are divided into nations, each of which conducts its affairs in a spirit of justice and law.* Ultimately such individual and collective responsibility will establish the Kingdom of God on earth through the abolition of national rivalries and war.

God is the central character of the drama. He is represented as having created the world with all that is in it for the sake of man, and as having created man to glorify Him. That assumption, which underlies traditional religion, clarifies what the biblical writings meant to their authors and contemporaries. The following scriptural statements are a few of hundreds which confirm this mythological version of human history.

The anonymous prophet who foretold the restoration of the exiled Judeans refers to them as "the people whom God had formed for Himself that they might recount His praise (Isa. 43:21). The same prophet quotes God as saying: "For My name's sake I have been patient with you. For My honor's sake I have bridled My anger against you, so as not to cut you off" (*ibid.,* 48:9). And in the Song of Moses, which recites the epic of Israel's early career, God would have destroyed His people on account of their obstinacy and rebelliousness had He not feared lest their foes should say "it is our might that has triumphed" (Deut. 32:26–27). Likewise the Psalmist praises God for shepherding him and leading him in the paths of righteousness for the sake of His own name (Ps. 23:3).

Thus the Bible asserts that God governs mankind and directs

the panorama of creation for the sake of His own name and glory. Furthermore, the entire course of nature and human history manifests His infinite power and inexorable justice—tempered by forgiving mercy. Since according to this premise every event in history reflects the power and justice of God, the biblical record of the people of Israel reveals a definite plan which gives purpose and meaning to those events.

The first eleven chapters of the Book of Genesis recount the events which preceded God's choice of Abraham as the founder of a nation to exemplify the function of Divinity and to maintain justice through law in human society (Gen. 18:17–19). Originally, God expected the entire human species to be governed by law analogous to that of the heavens above and the earth below. He expected man's implicit obedience, similar to the obedience exacted from the rest of creation. Man, however, displayed the tendency to live by a law of his own and to play the god. His rebellion is symbolized in the story of the Garden of Eden. The murder of Abel by Cain and the latter's subsequent disclaimer of responsibility unleash such lawlessness and violence that God is represented as regretting His creation of man (Gen. 6:7). He would have wiped out the entire human race had it not been for Noah and his family, who alone were considered worthy of being saved from doom.

Once again the human species displayed their recalcitrance against the will of God. Instead of spreading out over the earth as God had intended them to do (Gen. 1:28), they tried to build a megalopolis to probe the mysteries of Heaven and to challenge the sovereignty of God. But God frustrated their arrogance by confusing their language and dispersing them. Thus, according to the ancient mind, various nations with their rivalries for power came into being. By using some as rods against others, God would punish the sinful ones among them (Isa. 10:5–7).

God then sought to create a nation that would serve as a paradigm of justice through law in its way of life. Far from leaving its founder Abraham and his descendants to themselves, God is represented as helping them to carry out His purpose with mankind. While on the one hand He promised to bring them to a land flowing with milk and honey, He did not permit them to take possession of the Promised Land as long as "the measure of sin" of its inhabitants was not full. For several generations the proto-nation of Israel became bondmen in the land of Egypt. When, after being liberated from Egyptian bondage, they arrived in the Wilderness of Sinai, God revealed himself and gave them the laws which were to govern their lives.

Israel's career in the Wilderness and in the Promised Land is replete with incidents of rebellion against God's will. But although it adopted the ways of idolatrous nations, God, for His own name's sake, would not allow the nations to destroy Israel. He would make His Chosen People suffer exile and all manner of affliction so that they would repent. With the transformation of Israel's nature, the nature of mankind as a whole and the rest of creation would be transformed. The biblical philosophy of history defines hope for mankind in terms of God's transformation of human nature so that all mankind will come to obey His will.

This view is expressed in the two opening chapters of the Book of Isaiah, in which the prophet denounces Israel's transgression yet promises the establishment of God's Kingdom on earth. In God's name Isaiah cries out:

> I have reared, I have brought up sons, and they have rebelled against me. . . . Ah, sinful nation, a folk whose guilt is heavy, ah race of wrongdoers, sons degenerate. . . . They have abandoned the Lord and spurned the Majesty of Israel . . . Had not the Lord of hosts left us a few to survive, we would have fared like Sodom, no better than Gomorrah [Isa. 1:2, 4, 9].

But, assuming Israel's repentance, he concludes: "I will restore your rulers as at first and your counsellors as in the beginning, and afterwards you shall be called 'The stronghold of justice, the faithful city' " (ibid., 26). The second chapter prophesies the age of universal peace when God will help the people of Israel to achieve ethical nationhood and will impel other nations to achieve international peace.

Thus from the beginning of mankind's history to its culmination with the establishment of God's Kingdom on earth the

Bible conceived history as a revelation of God's purpose with mankind. History was not regarded as a progressive evolution of the human species through its own conscious efforts to rise above what it has in common with the subhuman. When man's knowledge of the universe was geocentric and his conception of God was anthropomorphic, primitive wisdom was theocentric. Its theology spoke in terms of man's relevance to God as a means to God's prestige. But if modern man accepts the scientific implications of science from Copernicus to the astronauts, he must realize that heaven is empty space. Only on earth is God relevant to man as the cosmic Power that makes for his salvation. Whereas in pre-modern religion nature was personified, modern man is treated as part of depersonified nature. The first step in maturation which wisdom, wedded to science, achieved was taken by Spinoza. His formula *Deus sive natura* made God and nature synonymous; but Spinoza evaded the problem of evil by treating it as outside the realm of objective or scientific reality.

The average thinking Jew is in a predicament. Although he values Jewish identity, he cannot subscribe to the mythological version of biblical philosophy of history. Rejecting the anthropomorphic idea of God, he has become not merely an agnostic, but an *ignostic*. He does not know what the word "God" means. The biblical philosophy of history assumes man's relevance or importance to God. Modern man must experience God's relevance to man. An authentic conception of God is relevant to the facts of human nature and to the contemporary world. God as the Power in nature and in the human species that makes for the salvation of men and nations gives purpose and meaning to their existence.

In the biblical account, the God of Israel created and ordered the world according to the laws of nature and created the people of Israel to live according to the laws of the Torah (cf. Ps. 19). Since both the laws of the Torah and those of physical nature are treated in the Bible as manifestations of *divine wisdom*, explicit homogeneity is implied between Nature and Nature's God (cf. Prov. 9 and Job 28). This conception *negates* the notion that belief in God is purely subjective, that it does not affirm the existence of a cosmic process. The cosmic process of universal reciprocity outside the human mind comes to be God only when it is experienced as cosmic interdependence, and, in the human world, as moral responsibility. God's relevance to man consists in impelling him so to control and direct his strivings as to satisfy all his life needs without reversion to strife and war.

The term "God" does not belong to the category of objective facts which are the subject matter of *reason* and *intelligence*. It belongs to the category of *values* which, as spiritual *factors*, are the subject matter of *wisdom*. Particularly in the Bible, wisdom refers to the experience and scale of values which answer man's vital needs.

How shall modern man reconstruct the traditional conception of God? Neither through mysticism nor reason, but through the emotional experience of responsibility can we become aware of His existence as the Power that assures man's fulfillment and survival. The mounting peril of human extinction through war can be averted only if the nations conduct their political and economic activities in the spirit of ethical nationhood. In the ancient mythological world Israel was expected to learn that lesson and to exemplify it among the other nations.

The Bible supports the reinterpretation of the belief in God in terms of human conduct that is godlike, creative and founded on justice through law. Thus, in mythological idiom, the Bible relates: "YHWH saw how great was man's wickedness on earth, and how every plan devised by his mind was nothing but evil all the time. And YHWH regretted that He had made man on earth and His heart was saddened" (Gen. 6:5–6). Demythologized, man's sin of irresponsibility culminating in violence, if unpunished, would not only disprove God's omnipotence, it would deny His very existence. The Rabbinic tradition confirms this version of the belief in God as dependent on the behavior of man. The Rabbinic comment on "You are my witnesses, says YHWH" (Isa. 43:10) reads: "If you are my witnesses, I am God; if you are not my witnesses, I am not, so to speak, God" (*Yalkut Shimeoni* quoting *Sifré* and commenting in the same spirit upon three additional texts). Mature wisdom or authentic religion *depends upon faith in man*. The reality of God can be experienced only when mankind acts in a way that makes for its creative survival.

Civilization is in greater danger than ever before because both the nuclear powers and the smaller nations conduct international relations on a level of moral irresponsibility. The very survival of mankind demands the modification of absolute sovereignty in the direction of ethical nationhood. From the very beginning that has been the purpose and meaning of Jewish existence.

The foregoing throws new light upon the traditional Jewish doctrine of the Jews as God's Chosen People. In the same manner as the sages of old interpret Israel's being God's witnesses, modern thought interprets the second half of the verse in Isaiah: "and my servant whom I have chosen." Israel would indeed prove to be God's Chosen People, were it to function as God's servant; but, by its own admission in Sacred Scriptures and in its liturgies, Israel is far from having actually served God.

3.   WHAT GOD MEANS TO MAN

The subjective experience of Godhood through moral responsibility or conscience presupposes a high degree of ethical development and requires lifelong and intensive education of conscience. The need to be needed—as true of nations as of individuals—is the objective psychological experience behind the need to be accepted and loved. We love what we need; to be needed is to be loved. Possessive love, which is self-centered, differs from creative love, which is community-centered and is implied in the behest: "You shall love the Eternal your God" (Deut. 6:7).

To be needed a person must be honest, creative, just and ever ready to serve. His creativity need not be of a high intellectual, esthetic or technical order. To the extent that a person produces more than he consumes, he is creative. He augments the positive values that make life worthwhile for the generality of mankind. Such is the wisdom, or sense of spiritual values, which public religion should foster.

If the purpose and meaning of humanization is to render individuals and nations fit to survive, the ultimate question is, *What constitutes fitness?* Men and nations must experience the need to be needed and have the opportunity and the capacity to fulfill that need. That criterion for the distinction between good and evil harmonizes with cosmic or transhuman forces. It is not the product of man's arbitrary will. Not man, but nature's God is the measure.

The myth concerning the tree of knowledge of good and evil may be interpreted to the effect that man's destiny is subject to cosmic rather than human forces. In trying to play the god by becoming a law unto himself, independent of the cosmic process of reciprocity, man ultimately resorts to violence and invites destruction. Man's career on earth reflects his disregard of "God's way of justice through law." Had man submitted to divine law he might have achieved the goal of universal peace. Man's fate now hangs in the balance. Will he acquire enough wisdom to choose life?

The message of Judaism as *wisdom*, which went out to the Jewish people, is of tremendous import to the rest of the world. *The universal reciprocity which functions as nature's God should become manifest in the moral responsibility of men and nations through commitment to ethical nationhood.* If man is to avert cataclysm, he must control his lusts and aggressions and obey the cosmic law as first adumbrated in Israel's Torah. Referring to the European nations as "the sensitive center of world power that could unleash forces of incalculable destruction," George W. Ball states:

> they have got us all in trouble before, and they have a special responsibility for staying out of trouble again, but to do so, they must take counsel from a bloody history and put aside the corrosive national rivalries of the past. This means more than a change of heart. It requires the institutionalizing of that change of heart through a modern political structure [*The Discipline of Power*, p. 19].

We ignore Divinity at our peril, declared the prophets and psalmists. They based their own insights upon revelation; in the age of the computer and space capsule, man must strive to regain belief in nature's God. Only then can he reconcile the scientific discoveries of anthropology, sociology and psychology with humanist religion and rediscover the spiritual insights of the past.

The Irrelevance of Theodicy

If God, conceived as function, denotes whatever is of ultimate value to mankind, He cannot be represented as a personal Being infinite in power and in goodness, which is a contradiction in terms. Hence all theodicies which claim to justify God's ways to man are inconsistent and meaningless. Nature is infinite chaos, with all its evils forever being vanquished by creativity, which is God as infinite goodness. That is the conclusion arrived at through wisdom that is mature. The power of God is inexhaustible but not infinite.

The Hebrew Bible portrays God as dispensing retributive justice, tempered albeit with mercy. This unqualified assumption of the Pentateuchal Torah and *Ketuvim* (Writings), which comprise the Book of Psalms, is confirmed by virtually all the prophets with the possible exception of Habakkuk and Jeremiah. The latter, in an atypical passage, complains: "Why does the way of the wicked prosper? Why do all the faithless live in comfort?" (Jer. 12:1). On the whole, Jeremiah admonishes man to forego pride in his own strength, wealth and wisdom and to rely on God's practice of justice and righteousness on earth (*ibid.*, 9:23–24). Habakkuk, in despairing mood, also rebukes God: "Wherefore doest Thou gaze upon faithless men and keep silent when the wicked swallows up him that is more righteous than himself?" (Hab. 1:13).

But one must peruse Job and Koheleth to find a sustained and forthright challenge of the normative Jewish tradition that happiness is the reward of virtue and of trust in God. Rejecting the reproaches of his "comforters," Job insists: ". . . it is God who has undone me; I cry for help and get no justice" (Job 19:6–8). Finally, after a score of chapters, God rebukes Eliphaz for his dishonest sycophancy and upholds the sufferer's honest doubt: "My anger is hot against you and your two friends, for, unlike My servant Job, you have not told the truth about me" (*ibid.*, 42:7).

In the wisdom book Ecclesiastes, Koheleth avers: "All manner of things I have seen in my fleeting life; the good man perishing by his very goodness and the evil man flourishing upon his evil" (Eccles. 7:15). "There is no evil like this in the world, that all men have one fate . . . for just and unjust, the good, bad and pure and impure, for him who sacrifices and for him who never sacrifices" (*ibid.*, 9:23). But in the end even that skeptic feels compelled to mitigate the harshness of his reflections: ". . . stand in awe of God, obey His commands: that is everything for every man. For in judging all life's secrets God will have every single thing before Him to decide whether it is good or evil" (*ibid.*, 12:13–14).

This modification of unreflective conformity to conventional faith does not solve the problem of evil but treats it as a *mystery* which man, because of his limited understanding, cannot fathom. Human beings must not apply to God the same criteria of right and wrong, of justice and injustice, as to their fellowmen. "My plans are not like your plans, nor your ways like my ways, so the Lord declares; nay, as heaven is higher than the earth, so are my ways higher than your ways, and My plans than your plans" (Isa. 55:8–9). Accordingly Job is reproached for questioning God's justice.

With the rise of Pharisaism the Jews acquired a new world outlook. They attempted to reconcile the contradictions between traditional faith and disquieting fact through the belief in an hereafter. There the inequities of this world—the unrewarded merits of the righteous and the unpunished sins of the wicked— would be rectified. Until the eighteenth century faith in post-mortem justice kept Jews, Christians and Moslems loyal to their respective religions.

Submission and resignation have prevailed throughout the centuries. During the Rabbinic period Rabbi Jannai alone voiced man's incapacity to cope with evil. "It is not in our power to express either the prosperity of the wicked or the affliction of the righteous" (*Pirke Avot*, IV:19). Yossel Rakover, a martyr who perished in the Warsaw Ghetto, declared, "I believe in the God of Israel, even though He has done everything to destroy my belief in Him. I believe in His laws even though I cannot justify his ways . . . I bow before His majesty, but I will not kiss the rod with which He chastises me" (Zvi Koletz, *Yossel Rakover Speaks to God*).

The most ingenious attempts to reconcile the tragic condition of mankind with the traditional conception of an almighty, all-perfect supernatural Being are futile. A rational conception of God renders theodicies superflous and irrelevant. The Bible itself provides precedent for questioning traditional assumptions. Viewed as a dynamic and evolving religious civilization Judaism answers such questions with modern assumptions which should not be regarded as final or authoritative.

Although the great monotheistic religions called upon man to live in accordance with moral law, they have failed because of their misconception of the God idea. A relevant conception of God might have dissuaded some great thinkers from rejecting religion. Witness Karl Marx who made a god out of the industrial process; Nietzsche who heralded the death of God; and Freud who "interred" religion as illusion. The very processes in nature and in man that function creatively and that make for fulfillment should be identified as God or Divinity. God is not a supernatural Being who metes out rewards and punishments and whose inexplicable acts must be reconciled with the prosperity of the wicked and the sufferings of the righteous. All human evil should be countered by the human striving for self-fulfillment and against the destructive forces in man and nature.

Tradition, as *immature* wisdom, has misled the human mind. It assumed that God was a supernatural Being existing outside nature whose laws He could at any time suspend to perform miracles. Creativity was assumed to belong only to God. Man was forbidden to rely on his own understanding and initiative. Knowledge, which conferred power, was a prerogative of priests and their priestly ancestors who derived their authority from God. Hence traditional religion was obsessed by neophobia, the fear of the new and the untried. Galileo was imprisoned in his own house for life because he declared that the earth moved around the sun. Man must assert his own creativity in harmony with the creativity that is in the cosmos in order to counter the evils in nature and in himself. But that attitude, which encourages man to share the prerogative of creativity with God must be controlled, lest it be used by man to play God.

Man's creative powers are engaged in his self-improvement and in his service to society. He is creative when he combats evil in his own nature, such as the greed which leads to exploitation, aggression and war. The humblest chore performed conscientiously contributes to human betterment and therefore to cosmic creativity. To be sure, there is entropy and there is death and worlds are being destroyed; but the process of creativity goes on simultaneously. To the extent that human beings live and act creatively, as they do when they subject their interpersonal and intergroup behavior to "justice which is spelled out into law," they function as partners with nature's God—the creative process of the cosmos.

Wisdom is evolutionary, not static. Any theodicy which conceives of God as a supernatural and personal Being who watches over every individual and metes out rewards or punishment is incompatible with the facts of life. Proof of the existence of God does not inhere in attempts to justify His ways with man. Such theodicy is irrelevant and untenable.

Conscience does not philosophize or theologize concerning the problem of evil in the world. Conscience is the pain of the human spirit. *Its function is not to give man information about God or to reconcile Him to life with all its evils, but to help man combat natural and man-made evils that mar human life.* "Abstinence from misconduct is not enough. Indifference to corruption anywhere in the community is also guilt" (Pronouncement of the General Board of the National Council of Churches, adopted in 1951).

The law of moral creativity and responsibility does not reduce religion to ethical culture. The worship of God in religion is not directed toward a Being who rewards and punishes, but to the creative Power in the cosmos and in ourselves as individuals and as members of nations. That Power brings order out of endless chaos and good out of actual and potential evil. It is therefore necessary to transform the conventional type of worship. Instead of verbose adoration, worship should retain from the traditional prayers those sections which express what God has meant to the Jewish people in the past, supplemented by meditations and petitions which relate the role of conscience to current problems. Public worship should concern itself mainly with the improvement of character and conduct in the individual and in society.

Jewish tradition assigns to the study of Torah a high spiritual value (cf. *Misnah, Peah,* I). As a result of non-Jewish religious influence and the natural entropy of spiritual values, that tradition has eroded. Non-Jewish influences in the modern treatment of the *Kaddish* have transmuted a prayer of adoration by those who had regaled themselves in the study of the Torah into a magic formula for redeeming the souls of the departed from the torments of *Gehinnom.*

The spiritual renewal of Jewish life depends upon a revival of the study of Torah. Focusing on man-made evils, religion should involve the whole of mankind in the creation of a world society in which all conflicts would be resolved, not by violence, but by negotiation and law.

Rabbi Alan W. Miller has ably summarized the irrelevance of theodicy as follows:

> In the first or this-world period of Jewish religion the question "Why does a man suffer?" could only be answered by "Because he is wicked" or "Because his father or grandfather was wicked." On the other hand, in the otherworldly post-biblical period (Post-Maccabeean and Rabbinic), the question "Why does a man suffer?" could be answered in one of several ways. It could mean, in the simple sense of an ancient theory, that he was wicked. It could also mean that he was righteous and was suffering either because God loved him (the potter only tests the best pots) or because he was paying off in this world for his few sins, so that he might enjoy a life of uninterrupted bliss in the world to come. With such theological "epicycloids," the Jew survived up to the Age of Auschwitz.
>
> It has been suggested that Auschwitz presents a unique and unprecedented challenge to the concept of reward and punishment. This is an understatement of the problem. All human suffering which makes any suggestion that an Akiba, whose skin was flayed off by the Romans, or any of our

latter day saints, who surely suffered no less intensely, must endure punishment in this world that they might enjoy bliss in the next, is totally unacceptable to the modern mind.

It is to avoid such theological absurdities that we must adopt the religio-humanist conception that human suffering is due neither to the eclipse of God, nor to the will of God (conceived as a Person). Suffering is due either to man's failure, either willful or unconscious, to reckon with the physical or biological laws of nature, or with those moral laws of responsibility, which are an extension of the cosmic process of universal reciprocity, and which are divine, insofar as they make for man's creative survival. Polarity, the principle of independence and interdependence, the idea that everything which exists is itself but at the same time is inextricably related to everything else, which operates in the sphere of physical objects as gravity, operates in the sphere of human society as Divinity when it is consciously recognized as such.

In the spirit of the prophets, religious humanism sees ethical behavior, responsibility in action within society, as a prime Revelation of God. In this we agree with the prophets. But, the prophets were right for the wrong reasons, right to affirm that society must be ethical, wrong in affirming that a Heavenly King uses Assyria as a "rod of His anger," to punish infractions of the ethical imperative. German society permitted itself to degenerate into a godless society. *Where men fail to cooperate with that cosmic principle of independence and interdependence, which spells human responsibility on an interpersonal and collective scale, Auschwitz can occur.*

A bridge breaks down in the middle of a storm and countless innocent lives are hurled into oblivion. Thornton Wilder in his *The Bridge of San Luis Rey* may attempt to find a "theological" justification for such a tragedy, but we know that the problem is to build bridges which will not break down.

CHAPTER III

Nature's God as the Source
of Moral Law

THE Sages of the Talmud, whose outlook was unqualifiedly revelationist, suggested that the conduct of some animals embodied lessons for man. Quoting Job's extolment of God, "He causes us to learn from the land animals, and to gather wisdom from the birds of heaven" (Job 35:11), the Sages commented: "If the Torah had not been given us, we might have learned modesty in mating from the cat, chastity from the dove, honesty from the ant, and good manners from the rooster" (*Eruvin* 100b). Jewish medieval theologians also sought guidance for moral and religious behavior in the natural functioning of the human mind. In their view man might derive authentic knowledge of God and His laws by giving credence to his instincts and experience. Since the Torah upholds the natural order of which man's experience is a part, the spirit of Jewish tradition confirms the role of nature in man's quest for the knowledge of God. Thus *naturalism might well serve as a source of morality*.

It is clear that the moth-eaten philosophical "proofs" for the existence of God—whether ontological, cosmological or teleological—are as irrelevant to human behavior as are estimates of the number of light years between the stars of the Milky Way and the earth. Irrelevant, too, is the abstract God of deism, a philosophy which pretends to be religion but which treats God as "emeritus." Rejecting the belief that God has revealed

Himself through the spoken word, or through human incarnation, modern-minded men can arrive at a demythologized conception of God. That conception derives from those laws of nature or world order which impel man to make the most creative use of his life and his world. The marshaling and analysis of accurate data have established a scientific basis for important conclusions with regard to the human condition. Just as the uniform operation of the natural law under ever-changing conditions eventuates in the conception of creative evolution, so the naturalist conception of God which underlies ethical religion can vouchsafe creative human development and save mankind from extinction. Whitehead's principle that "the basis of all authority is the supremacy of fact over thought" applies to religion as well as to science (A. N. Whitehead, *The Function of Reason*, p. 64).

The naturalist moral law, no less than the naturalist *God idea*, is a far cry from both the supernaturalist-revelational and the philosophical-rational concepts. According to Kant's classic formulation, the moral law bears the same relation to the actual practice of morality as the categories of the understanding bear to the rational knowledge of the world of nature. His categorical imperative is an underived law of practical reason: "Act only on that maxim whereby thou canst at the same time will that it should become a universal law." Kant based the moral law solely upon the *reasoning* of the human mind. However, it is preferably to be inferred from natural law, and therefore regarded as inevitable in its functioning. Insofar as such functioning makes for the moralization and full humanization of man it is divine from the standpoint of what God should mean to man—as the Power that makes for mankind's creative survival. This realization would eliminate from traditional religion its immature and absurd tenets concerning God as meting out rewards and punishments and as arbitrarily designating some human beings for eternal bliss and others for eternal damnation.

What in human experience is common to those human laws which are termed moral or ethical? Wherein is that common element a manifestation of natural or cosmic law? The moral law through which man strives to attain his self-fulfillment is an extension of the law of polarity which operates in nature as a whole. Apart from man, nature does not act in a moral context. Moral law differs from the physical laws as the thunderous roar of Niagara Falls differs from the waters. But nature's neutrality does not remove moral law from empirical category.

The categorical authority of the moral law does not rely upon social convention nor is it derived from revelation or metaphysics. The moral law operates in man's yearning which, however vague and ineffable, is as demanding as the need for food, safety, health and mating. That yearning focuses on the need to be needed and its gratification through involvement with an organic group. Through close family relations, extended to his tribe and nation, the individual learns self-discipline as a means to his own and his group's survival.

The quest for food, safety and mating are manifestations of *consciousness* which subhumans have in common with man. The yearning for what one *ought* to be, feel or do is a manifestation of *self-consciousness* of which only the human being is capable. This self-consciousness is as much a part of nature as instinct, or the subpersonal. The moral law corresponds to the natural law of polarity of independence and interdependence that operates in the cosmos. The sense of duty or responsibility expressed in moral or ethical behavior combines the individual's self-conscious operation of both selfhood and otherhood, of independence and interdependence, of freedom and law. These manifestations of universal polarity are not separate and conflicting trends which exist as such only in man's self-consciousness. Everything, from the infinitesimal entity to that of inconceivable magnitude, is simultaneously cause and effect, self-active and interactive, independent and interdependent.

Everything that exists is in a state of tension between these two polar trends. That tension, passing through man's self-consciousness—with his powers of memory, imagination, abstraction, reason and intelligence—must cope with his sense of duty or responsibility. When a person follows the dictates of duty or responsibility, his inner tension is resolved. Contrary to revelationist doctrine, the moral law does not emanate from the commands of a supernatural divinity, nor is it solely based on the Kantian and rationalist category of practical reason. Moral law is an extension of natural law, as reflected in man's sense of responsibility and in his empirically validated behavior. Self-consciousness acts as a process of refraction. It refracts responsibility toward its two poles. The pole of self-activity accentuates freedom to choose among alternative courses of action. The pole of interactivity urges with the compulsiveness of inherent "necessity." Both poles operate with the inevitability of cosmic law.

Moral responsibility is built into our capacities as human beings. Insofar as it is requisite for individual fulfillment and for the creative survival of the human species, it emanates from the Power in nature that makes for salvation, or from nature's God. Albert Schweitzer wrote: "My life is completely and unmistakably determined by the mysterious experience of God revealing Himself within me as ethical will and desiring to take hold of my life" (Letter to Oscar Kraus, 1923, quoted by Carl Herman Voss in the *Saturday Review*, April 7, 1962).

Many scientists and philosophers glory in their aloofness from social issues. The logical positivists describe ethical values and moral standards as emotive and hence lacking objective status as verifiable propositions. Recently a change of attitude has surfaced at academic gatherings and in scientific literature. "An ever-increasing number of physical scientists are awakening to their social responsibility. They not only worry about the uses to which the new formidable technology may be put; they warn the leaders of an impending catastrophe in store for *all*, if the gifts of knowledge are turned into weapons of violence" (Anatol Rapoport, *Science and the Goals of Man*, p. iii).

Without some freedom of choice man could not develop responsibility for his thoughts and actions. Yet freedom—except in an imaginary social vacuum—is limited by determinist factors such as heredity, environment and a succession of previous choices which may be habit-forming. Philosophic dualists attempt to resolve this conflict by assigning freedom and necessity to disparate areas of the mind. Necessity or fact is ascribed to practical reason; freedom or value is attributed to pure reason; and never the twain shall meet. Monists achieve theoretical oneness by dismissing freedom of choice as an illusion. But if free will were inauthentic and unreal no one could be held responsible for his conduct and the social order would collapse.

The human experience of responsibility *embodies the natural process of polarity* which, though not analyzable, is no illusion. Spinoza held that freedom, upon which responsibility is predicated, is not only compatible with causality but presupposes its existence. And Abraham Kaplan wrote: "The working of causality does not set limits to human freedom, but, on the contrary, gives man's freedom a purchase on reality. That man is free does not mean that he stands outside the causal network, but that the causes working on him work through him, that is, *through his knowledge of causes and effects*" (*The New World of Philosophy*, p. 250).

The all inclusive, moral imperative posits mutual responsibility of individuals within each group, of the group as a whole to each of its members and of groups to one another. It is natural and ethical for the sense of mutuality, which functions superconsciously in every normal human being, to be experienced intensively among those who are part of the same social organism and most intensively among those who are part of the same concentric social organisms.

The totalitarian threat to moral responsibility stems from an authoritarianism whose absolute power robs men and nations of freedom and moral responsibility. Blind, unquestioning and uncritical obedience obliterates the main human differentia—moral responsibility. Vladimir I. Rakovsky, a Communist author, who was tried because he led a protest against the Soviet Union's treatment of writers, defended himself by putting communism on trial. Rakovsky pleaded:

> I have before me the text of the Soviet Constitution: "In accordance with the interests of the workers and with the aim of strengthening the Socialist system, the citizens of the U.S.S.R. are guaranteed by law . . . the right of street processions and demonstrations. . . ." Where is this right denied? In Madrid . . . I see a disturbing identity between fascist Spanish and Soviet legislation.

Rejecting Rakovsky's plea, the prosecutor said: "The accused is abusing the right for a final statement. He criticizes the laws, discredits the activities of the organs of the Committee of State Security (KGB) . . ." (*The New York Times*, December 27, 1967).

Although latent, the sense of moral responsibility is as universally built into human nature as is the sense of interdependence. However men may differ, they share a sense of common destiny. They desire creative human survival whose attainment depends upon the individual's freedom of choice among various courses of action. By playing upon man's fears and hopes, by alternating threats of hell and rewards of heaven, many religious institutions have sacrificed man's sense of human interdependence and social responsibility to his egocentric drives.

The 879-page *Oxford Book of Quotations* includes only one item on "responsibility"; the 2,812-page *Home Book of Quotations* none. The twelve-volume *Encyclopedia of Religion and Ethics* contains one brief article restricted to Christ's teaching of responsibility. The item "responsibility" like that of "value" is conspicuously absent from the *Synopticon*. Thus a basic ethico-religious concept is ignored or treated cursorily in voluminous catalogues of human thought.

The implications of moral responsibility for creative human survival are involved and complex. It will take many a revolution in the organization of human society and in its forms of government before moral responsibility becomes effective. The main prerequisites to its functioning are (1) that every mature human being should realize that his actions affect the well-being and competence of all within the range of the concentric groups to which he belongs, and (2) that the political leaders of these concentric groups should administer their public affairs with a view to goodness rather than greatness. Out of the normative functioning of moral responsibility would emerge ethical nationhood, which should become the goal of the United Nations. To hold in check the unlimited power of destruction which has come into man's possession, nations must relinquish some aspects of absolute sovereignty. They must renounce war as an instrument for resolving conflicting interests and disputes.

Human beings, by virtue of their interdependence and independence, are mutually responsible for one another's honesty, justice, compassion, loyalty, knowledge, competence, creativity, courage and faith. Mutual responsibility, on the personal, national and international levels, requires the maintenance of justice, freedom and good will. Those political objectives reflect the functioning, on a human level, of the natural laws of polarity. Freedom relates to the pole of independence; justice, to the pole of interdependence; and good will, to the synthesis, or balanced functioning, of the two.

Institutional religion should foster these primary moral traits:

1. *Honesty* is a primal virtue whose demands cannot be modified to accommodate a particular culture or civilization. Although qualitative degrees and relativism do not apply to the rigid standards of honesty, situations may arise which mitigate the obligation to speak out. Whether or not a physician should tell the truth to his incurable patient may involve psychological and therapeutic factors which outweigh the obligatory character of full and frank disclosure.

Cynics maintain that the clergy are not expected to express their honest opinions on matters of religion. That politicians and advertising copywriters do not speak the unvarnished truth is taken for granted. But if religious leaders condone dishonesty, all their efforts to foster the other virtues lack credence and confidence.

Honesty is basic not because it is the best policy. Honesty, reduced to the level of enlightened self-interest, whether personal or national, violates the cosmic process of polarity; it is against nature. The moral law upholds regard for reality and eschews self-delusion. Man's safeguarding of his own integrity is an extension into human consciousness of coherence in the world order. In international relations dishonesty inhibits world peace. Within the nation it robs the individual of freedom and moral responsibility. Totalitarianism, as Karl Jaspers points out, bases its entire regime on "the principle of the lie" (*The Future of Mankind*, p. 106).

The lie, which totalitarianism has elevated into a principle, serves democracy when it is pragmatically unprincipled. Many Americans serving abroad who are receptive to flattery, bribes and other preferment contribute to the low esteem in which the

United States, as the exponent of democracy, is held. Denouncing the Vietnam adventure, Senator J. W. Fulbright referred to the "credibility gap" between the realities of the situation in Vietnam and the reports issued by the United States government.

2. *Justice* envisages authentic equality in all human relations. The operation in nature of distributive justice as equality may be observed in the life cycle of a tree, which nourishes its leaves which in turn sustain the tree. To the extent that mutual dependence operates in nature, it aids animate beings to survive. Self-consciousness in man which sets boundaries between selfhood and otherhood accentuates assertiveness and selfishness at the expense of justice. In the last analysis, human survival may depend upon the establishment of a balance between ego and other drives, which is justice.

Reinhold Niebuhr writes,

> The democratic world has long since learned that the residual egotism of man makes an element of coercion in the community necessary. But price in justice for the boon in order will be too high, if every center of authority is not brought under public scrutiny and control, and if every center of power is not balanced by some other center of power. An equilibrium of power is in fact the first prerequisite of justice. The Marxist dream of justice has turned into a nightmare of injustice, because the Marxist Utopia established a monopoly of power. A series of miscalculations was responsible for this development [*Biblical Faith and Socialism in Religion and Culture*, p. 53].

3. *Compassion* or empathy prompts man not merely to feel *with* his neighbor, but to feel *as* he does. The ethical formula for compassion—"put yourself in the other person's place"—has not as yet turned up in any of the world's sacred writings. The nearest approach occurs in a Rabbinic treatise compiled at the end of the second century: "Do not judge your fellowman until you have put yourself in his place" (*Mishnah, Avot*, II, 4). Pragmatically, that precept, in negative form, should evoke the same mental and moral compassion as does the positive formula. An early biblical behest for compassion admonishes: "You shall not oppress a stranger; you know the heart of a

stranger, for you were strangers in the land of Egypt" (Exod. 23:9).

Like honesty, compassion hews to the line of reality. Man must know his neighbor, not as imagination—prompted by prejudice, embittered by envy or misled through ignorance—might paint him, but as his neighbor really is. All men are molded by heredity, environment and other factors. Although the human being readily forgives himself, he finds less reason to forgive others.

4. *Loyalty* toward one's religious group and the group's moral influence upon its adherents set into motion a constant and beneficent two-way passage between the individual and his organic society. The latter as a living organism achieves self-perpetuation through the mutual responsibility of its constituents. Similarly, the individual cannot exist in a vacuum. His personality and maturation depend upon sustained interaction with others who, in close association, develop a common language, a way of life and value structure. A self-perpetuating group— whether clan, tribe, nation or church—attains self-awareness through loyalty to a common religion. Although the nature gods of polytheism were imagined to minister to men's specific needs, one supreme deity, Osiris, Re or Jupiter, by extending hegemony over gods and men, fostered the continuity and collective consciousness of their respective worshipers. In ancient Israel YHWH represented the spirit of the people. In Rabbinic Judaism the Shekinah (Presence of God) manifested His impelling force as the collective consciousness of the Jewish people. "The Shekinah accompanied the Jews to wherever they were exiled" (*Megillah* 29b).

If an individual is to have a conscience, he must first become self-conscious as a person. His fulfillment as a person depends upon identification with an integrated society which inculcates an awareness of a common past and a sense of common destiny. Religion should foster this spirit of loyalty and mutual responsibility.

The foregoing description of loyalty represents an ideal situation where the group to which one belongs functions ethically— which is seldom the case. In actual life loyalty must take the form of the principle "My country right or wrong; if right, to be kept right; if wrong to be set right." None displayed greater loyalty than the ancient prophets who castigated their people mercilessly.

5. *Knowledge and intelligence.* The acquisition of knowledge, which a materialist would equate with power, is actually a *moral* duty. In its emphasis upon the *knowledge* of God, the Hebrew Bible defines recognition of His "way of justice through law." This basic tenet of traditional religion must be extended on moral grounds to encompass a *knowledge of reality and of physical and human nature.* Traditional believers who refuse to look into a telescope out of fear that their mythological notions about the universe would be shaken make a religion out of ignorance. As Montaigne observed: "nothing is so firmly believed as what is least known."

Knowledge of the world and man enables man to transcend the limitations of superstition and ignorance. It enhances his moral and spiritual powers. In Albert Schweitzer's words: "Man can control himself only if he understands both himself and the civilization he has created out of his longing for justice and peace." Comprehension of the evolutionary process in nature and of the role of the unconscious in human nature underlies the understanding of self and society. It proffers scientific standards to evaluate the authority of the past with balanced judgment concerning the future. Ethical religion advocates specific knowledge on the operation of polarity, organicity and creativity in the cosmos and in human life. Such knowledge is not an end in itself. Conceived as moral duty, it directs man's biological and psycho-social drives into creative and constructive channels.

If religion is ethical rather than a form of magic or theurgy, it must relate means to ends. It must set goals which are meaningful and exhort mankind to make his beliefs and commitments relevant to their attainment. Blind acceptance of religious dogmas and habit-propelled rituals are unethical. Anti-intellectualism or irrationalism, no matter how euphemistically disguised as intuitionism, romanticism or mysticism, distorts the truth and corrupts the sense of reality. Any conception of Divinity based upon delusion partakes of idolatry.

6. *Creativity* is a product of the interdependence of the individual and the world. In his creative contribution of thought, feeling and action man enhances personal and cosmic existence. Man should feel responsible for leaving the world not the worse but the better for having lived in it. Perhaps human survival and man's augmented power and knowledge testify to the predominance of creative over destructive forces.

Creativity, in consonance with the moral principle of service, fosters salvation, or fulfillment, in the process of living, not as an otherworldly reward which is extraneous to the striving for it. By marshaling all his resources for the performance of mundane as well as momentous tasks man lives creatively and experiences fulfillment. The experience of fulfillment and purposefulness in life motivates the development of other moral traits.

7. *Courage* in battle, natural disaster or other bodily peril is a self-evident validation of responsibility. Less evident as responsibility are the many acts of courage under circumstances of moral and mental stress. Illustrative of moral fortitude is the case of a young psychiatrist who, knowing that he was hopelessly ill, requested a trusted rabbi and friend to officiate at his funeral. He told the rabbi of his concern for his parents. His father had a heart condition. How would he take the blow? His wife, a physician, who was coping with grim reality, was helping him prepare their three very young children. He was also preparing his patients by referring them to another doctor.

When the rabbi asked his doomed friend how he managed to accept this tragedy with such courage, the latter explained: "If I am not strong, how can I expect those I love to carry on?" (*Dimensions of Jewish Existence*, B'nai B'rith Foundations, p. 28).

8. *Leadership*, in whose exercise are concentrated both good and evil potentialities, bears the chief responsibility for the fate of mankind. Mankind produced both a saintly Gandhi and a sadistic Hitler. The latter, with the assent of much of the "civilized world," nearly exterminated European Jewry and brought Western civilization to the brink of barbarism.

Responsibilities are crucial in the life of man. The conception of the Messiah as exercising supernatural powers reflects an abdication of responsibility on the part of both leader and disciple. Messianism implies a miracle-working God who suspends the laws of nature. Actually, in the same degree that God represents that syndrome of forces in nature that make for man's self-fulfillment, the Messiah represents those forces in man that make for self-realization.

Pope Paul's failure to recognize the responsibilities of leadership was assailed by Dr. John Rock, a leading Roman Catholic, who helped develop the revolutionary birth-control pill. Denouncing the papal encyclical's prohibition of all artificial forms of birth control, he declared: "I was surprised. I was scandalized. Given the transparency of the requirements of mankind, one hardly expected the avowed leader of Christianity to abdicate so completely responsibility for the ultimate welfare of all" (*The New York Times*, August 4, 1968).

If man perseveres in moral endeavors—despite their failure to bring immediate happiness and their immediate cost in suffering —his education from early youth should "decentralize the individual, and persuade him to abandon his spontaneous subjective and egocentric attitude, in order to lead him to reciprocity and (which is practically the same thing) objectivity" (Jean Piaget, "The Right to Education in the Modern World" in comment on Article 26 of the *Universal Declaration of Human Rights*). His pursuit of a moral life should be recognized as a contribution to mankind's survival and enhancement. Through free choice to live by that pursuit man evinces moral courage, through which the world may yet become the Kingdom of God.

In the context of human survival the moral traits which should pertain to individuals apply also to nations. Ethical nationhood requires a responsible citizenry whose choice of leaders reflects the high moral standards of both leaders and constituents.*

Although this exposition of moral traits is by no means exhaustive, it will suffice to indicate that moral responsibility—as the human counterpart of the natural law of polarity—establishes

---

* Chauvinism, which substitutes uncritical worship of country for that of God, is as deficient in responsibility as is religion. In 1898 during the Dreyfus controversy, André Gide declared: "If saving an innocent Dreyfus involves any injury to the French State, everything should be done to make Dreyfus guilty, so that France may remain unstained" (Quoted by Hayim Greenberg in *The Inner Eye*, p. 174).

reciprocal action and coordination between independence and interdependence.

The sense of moral responsibility inculcated by religion is four-dimensional. It should operate (1) mutually among the members of that society, (2) within the continuing society as a whole toward each individual member, (3) in each individual toward the self-perpetuating society as a whole, and (4) in relations among all self-perpetuating societies. The last dimension implies international responsibility. Ideally, a society should operate simultaneously in all the foregoing dimensions.

So far religion has emphasized only mutual responsibility among the members of the continuing community and the responsibility of each individual to his particular community. But religion's passivity with regard to the other social responsibilities has impeded its moral role even on an interpersonal level.

Religion has sensitized collective conscience to matters of cult and ritual in the worship of God who is represented as the patron and guardian of the tribe, nation or church. Although the Zoroastrian religion did not ignore morals, G. F. Moore wrote of its liturgy: "The exact performance of the rite (the preparation and offering of the Hasma) and the exact recitation of long texts in a dead language is the essential thing; so done, it is sure to be efficacious. It not only procures blessings from the gods, but reinforces the gods and gives them power to overcome hostile influence and work for good" (*History of Religions*, Vol. I, p. 390).

Had religion fostered an interpersonal and an intergroup conscience within each group, it might have been more effective in subordinating the worldly powers, particularly the collective power of society itself, to the four-dimensional law of moral responsibility. So far the religions of mankind, from primitive to advanced, have operated as instruments of corporate power. The established religions have concentrated on national or church unity by promoting the exclusive and competitive spirit of their adherents. They have intensified the *collective consciousness* of their respective followers at the expense of their *collective conscience*. Yet mankind's survival may well depend upon religion's fostering of moral conscience in all its dimensions.

Man depends for his life and well-being upon the corporate

powers which he shares with members of his organic community. In ancient times a religion unified the political, economic, cultural and social activities of a community. Social religion created organic communities through the public cult, and a system of customs and laws regulating interpersonal relations.

Traditional religion through its priests, prophets and people has regarded these natural tasks as emanating from supernatural sources. Now that the human mind can analyze and abstract from the complex of social life that moral aspect which impels man to fulfill himself as a human being, man is free to reject the supernaturalist aspects of traditional religion.

Socrates dealt with moral issues from a humanist point of view. His conception of justice, as interpreted by Plato in *The Republic*, envisaged the division of society into three functional groups to harmonize with the threefold nature of man. Its toilers, guardians and rulers (philosopher-kings) would correspond, respectively, with the volitional, emotional and intellectual capacities of human beings. Plato's humanist approach to moral problems robbed the human person of freedom. He was not free to choose his own career in life but was relegated to whatever status and function the governing bureaucracy decided upon. Plato's *Republic* advocated the "exposure" of unfit or unwanted infants and the rearing of its future rulers in state institutions, where they would be free of family interference (and love).

The validation of moral law derives neither from naive assumptions about the will of a personal God nor from traditional notions concerning the nature of man. Only nature's God can validate the ethical traits which help man to control his biological needs and worldly power in the interest of creative human survival. The supernaturalist view of *oughtness*, based on *arbitrary* notions concerning human nature, lacks rational and empirical proof. Human nature, including its immoral tendencies, is the extension of cosmic processes.

Ancient religion included principles of government, law and justice, ascribed directly or indirectly to various gods, or to one god. As the human mind discerned inherent natural sanctions behind those principles, those sanctions were identified as autonomous conscience. This recent development in man's spiritual life confirms his evaluative judgment. His power to distinguish between right and wrong is not instigated by social convention but by some power that transcends it. Moreover, that Power or voice of God inheres in his own person as well as in the cosmos; it is integral to the order of the universe. Conscience connotes the dictation to man of what he should do and induces remorse for failure. Conscience is semi-conscious intellectual effort to experience Divinity, without recourse to anthropomorphic terms, rational propositions or mystic ecstasy. *It is modern man's way of experiencing Divinity, provided, of course, it is experienced as a demand for justice, freedom and cooperation in accordance with the principle enunciated by Hillel* (Ethics of the Fathers I, 14).

When primitive societies became aware of individual differences and apprehensive that those differences might inhibit their cooperation for their common welfare, a sense of belonging asserted itself. The authoritarian state was reinforced by state religion with its totems, symbols and demand for strict uniformity within the cult. Today unprecedented development of sophisticated weaponry by arrogant national sovereignties will destroy mankind, unless human cooperation is achieved. *The growing differentiation among individuals and societies makes it all the more imperative that they be welded into organisms.* Unless the principle of cosmic organicity penetrates human consciousness, impelling it to conceive mankind as one, mankind will not attain that universal loyalty which Josiah Royce designated as "loyalty to loyalty."

In the past the sense of belonging and loyalty was expressed through religion. The identification of religion with faith, in the sense of faithfulness or loyalty, is psychologically valid. Such faithfulness communicates genuine, though intangible, experience; it designates fellowship among persons, or within a permanent social group. That kind of belonging redeems us from the devastating sense of alienation. Religion helps the human being overcome the fear of being alone, which, according to Aristotle, only a superhuman or a subhuman being can endure.

In ancient civilizations the collective consciousness was hypostasized or deified in a totem, fetish or potentate. Each religion would elevate its heroes, historic events and places, holy texts and myths into *sancta* which enhanced the organic group spirit. In the sense that communism exacts loyalty—based on the authority of its scriptures, its symbols and its cultist rituals—it can be considered a religion, although its god, historical material-ism, is a contradiction in terms. The cultivation of any virtue at the expense of others converts that virtue into a vice. The greatest threat to human survival emanates from the chauvinist national loyalties which ride roughshod over freedom, justice, intelligence and truth.

Why does loyalty pose that threat? Loyalty and responsibility are inseparable. Loyalty is love directed toward an organic group. Man learns to be morally responsible through his loyalty toward his family. From the family circle loyalty grows to embrace larger social groupings such as clans, tribes, cities, na-tions, churches and peoples. With the progress of civilization the social horizons of loyalty should grow ever wider.

Unfortunately, sovereign nations have erected walls to contain loyalty within their respective borders. From the pinnacle of absolute sovereignty nations are absolved from moral respon-sibility to mankind as a whole or to other nations. Thus, while each nation expects exemplary conduct on the part of its citizens, it defends what it regards as its own interests with the morals, manners and might of a Genghis Khan. The citizen's subordination of moral responsibility to the dictates of his nation, in payment, so to speak, for the loyalty he owes, "authenticates" each nation's claim to absolute sovereignty.

What is the outcome of the doctrine of absolute national sovereignty? Lust for power and uncontrolled aggression may trigger an escalating series of international wars in the course of which all life on this planet may perish. "The troubles of modern society," writes Bayard West in *Conscience and Society* (p. 150), "spring less from the individual self-assertiveness of its individual members than from its failure to master collective aggressiveness."

As long as mankind is subject to the absolute sovereignty of nations, its loyalties are biased and its moral responsibility is inhibited. Will national leaders take steps to limit sovereignty and submit disputes to international courts or a modified and more equitable United Nations? The ideal of God's sovereignty, with its hope for mankind's future, is part of the Jewish contribution to civilization. The *Shema* with its proclamation of the oneness of God implies the oneness of mankind. Jews should be reminded of that ideal every time they utter the benediction in which they are made aware of God as "the King of the universe."

If Jewish religion is to speak to our day, it must do so in the language of moral responsibility as embracing all of humanity. Judaism has always assumed that mankind was one, and acknowledged God as its supreme Sovereign and Lawgiver. Isaiah and Micah envisioned the time when all the nations would come to the God of Israel to adjudicate their conflicting interests and when they would beat their swords into plowshares and their spears into pruning hooks. That vision is anticipated with ecstasy by the Psalmist in the four chapters recited every Sabbath eve (Ps. 96–99). They foretell the moral revolution which will bring rejoicing to mankind:

> Proclaim among the nations that the Eternal is King; He steadies the world and rules the nations with equity. Let the heavens rejoice and the earth be glad; let the sea and all its fullness thunder praise. Let the earth and all it holds exult, let all trees of the forest sing for joy before the Eternal, for He comes. He comes to rule the earth, to rule the world with righteousness and peoples with His faithfulness [Ps. 96:10–13].

Life is intrinsically creative. Every living thing survives as long as it is able to absorb matter from the environment and transform that matter into the substance of its own body. Sub-human creatures, not being self-conscious, act out their will-to-live instinctively. Man, being self-conscious, transforms his instinctive life into the conscious will-to-live. Whatever he creates —whether it be in the form of keeping his body alive and in good health or in the form of building cities, nations or civilizations—he creates by dint of his conscious will to live and to make the most of life. As with the other categories of responsibility, so with the category of creativity: *what obtains in the world order as a whole, as a law of nature, is metamorphosed into a moral law.* To exercise creativity is a duty which man must obey if he is to actualize his latent potentialities.

To appreciate the extent to which the human mentality has undergone the process of evolution, it is well to bear in mind that, if pre-modern man by some chance invented something new, he ascribed that invention to divine inspiration. To invent something new with intent amounted to trespassing on divine prerogatives. The skill displayed by Bezalel and Oholiov in the building of the Tabernacle in the Wilderness is ascribed in the Book of Exodus to divine inspiration. The assumption that only God creates was sufficient to discourage all initiative in science and technics. As long as God was conceived as a being entirely above and beyond nature and as having revealed to man all that he needs to know and do, the acceptance of the *status quo* in every phase of life was considered an act of piety.

That attitude has been undergoing a radical change in recent centuries when man's creative potentialities have been given free rein. In some quarters this has led to the denial of God's existence and to human disorientation. The wiser procedure is to modify the pre-modern conception of God in order to reconcile it with human experience. The result of that procedure is the conception of man as an integral part of cosmic nature. The realization of his potentialities is an extension of tendencies or laws in the cosmos and constitutes the moral law of his being. They reveal the Godhood or Divinity of the cosmos.

Unfortunately, when man augmented his mastery of physical nature, his creative skills were enlisted in the service of war rather than peace. The scientists and technologists are at last beginning to realize that the ever-increasing automation of human activity is fraught with incalculable hazard. At a recent meeting of the American Association for the Advancement of Science, Dr. Richard W. Hamming of the Bell Telephone Laboratories stated that the computer revolution will outdo even the industrial revolution in its effect on human life. "The computer revolution should rather be compared with the Copernican or the Darwinian revolution, both of which greatly changed man's idea of himself and the world in which he lives. Computers can stimulate atomic explosions and rocket launchings, and design, develop and test, theoretically, inventions that do not physically exist."

Now as never before, the most urgent moral imperative is the outlawing of war and the limitation of armaments. As long as war is recognized as legal, society is bound to be immoral. A society that resorts to violence and cunning cannot expect its members to lead moral lives. Moral man is as inconceivable in an immoral society as a saint in the company of gangsters. Under those circumstances, public religion is likely to be a conscious or unconscious form of hypocrisy and idolatry. This is not the case because of man's original sin, which is a myth, but because of his inventiveness which is not directed by original virtue.

A concentrated effort should be made to transfer all leadership in science, politics and economics from the waging of war to the waging of peace. To wage peace involves the control of populations, economic aid to emerging nations and the raising of living standards everywhere. But practical measures will not suffice. All peoples need reeducation and rehabituation in moral and spiritual values free from dogmatism and intolerance.

If Jews are to accept the moral responsibility imposed by their own tradition—which commands them to choose life as a people—they should promote a new spiritual orientation. *Divinity is that aspect of the whole of nature, both in the universe and in man, which impels mankind to create a better and happier world and every individual to make the most of his own life.* Such a conception of the moral law coincides with the pietist's assumption that man should so act as to experience the presence of Divinity. In the words of the Psalmist: "Try and see that the Eternal is good. Happy the man that takes refuge in Him" (Ps. 34:9). The knowledge of God need not be based on revelational or philosophical tradition. *Personal and natural experience can well be the source of morality as morality can be the source of religion.*

Thus the concept *wisdom* as the system of values which are

indispensable to creative human survival opens up new horizons of human experience. Those new horizons enable us to realize the purpose and meaning of human existence through the authentic experience of moral responsibility as the manifestation of Divinity.

CHAPTER IV

What Is Man?

I. WHAT PSYCHOLOGY CAN LEARN FROM RELIGION

THE mythological story of creation in the opening chapter of the Bible recounts that God made man in His own image. Hence, if we wish to know God, we should study His reflection in the nature of man. According to Harry Stack Sullivan,

> a survey of the history of the meaning of man would spread before us . . . many views that represent what we now know man is not. Man is not a creature of instinct—the view of Aristotle and McDougall; of transcendental powers between or among which he may choose his allegiance—the medieval view rather sympathetic to Rank; of logic and its categorical opposites—Bacon and, in a way, Alfred Adler and Alfred Korzybski; of the evolution of social intellect—Comte and some mental hygienists; of racial fitness—de Gobineau and Fuehrer Hitler; of a conflict of society and one's instincts—Freud; or of the racial unconscious—Jung [*Conceptions of Modern Psychiatry*, p. 14].

No less critical of prevailing views of human psychology Joseph Wood Krutch asked: "Can anyone deny that for at least a hundred years we have been prejudiced in favor of every theory, including economic determinism, mechanistic behaviorism, and relativism, that reduced the stature of man, until he ceases to be man at all in any sense that the humanists of an earlier generation would recognize?" (*American Scholar*, Summer 1967). Common to all such misconceptions of human nature is the reductionist fallacy which would reduce all psychological terms to physiological events or processes. Religion, conceived as wisdom, which is the art of "seeing life steadily and seeing it whole," should counteract the tendency to apotheosize or glorify the reductionist method of the physical sciences.

In the physical sciences reductionism is a valid method of arriving at desired technological purposes. Without the reductive method the range of technics would be limited. Applied to biology and particularly to psychology and other human sciences, reductionism is fallacious and misleading. Reducing all ethical values to economic factors has confined man's political and social life within the doctrinaire strait jacket of the class struggle.

Group religion as an anthropological, psycho-social phenomenon illumines many aspects of human conduct. As a system of belief and behavior, religion unites a nation, a people or a church. Religion creates a sense of belonging and fellowship among the members of a community. It helps the individual achieve self-fulfillment and happiness through the fostering of his potentialities and opportunities.

Depth psychology stresses the domination of the individual by his unconscious. It reveals the inhibitions that prevent the full assertion of his own individuality, particularly the obstructive aspects of his social environment. Yet therapy should evoke the helpful and creative forces in the cultural environment. Self-control and inner direction require self-discipline, all of which presuppose individual involvement in community life.

What is the function of authentic religion in fostering the creative survival of the human species? From the crude and grotesque notions of primitive group religions the concepts of God have matured, in keeping with the maturation of the social and cultural experiences of their adherents. However morally harmful their ascription of divinity or holiness to objects and persons, such groups have not lacked a sense of divinity or holiness. Without that awareness man is handicapped; he cannot become fully human. To lack a sense of the holy is to be unaware of or indifferent to the human differentia. Group religion in all its forms represents man's groping efforts to achieve that dynamic equilibrium in the satisfaction of his needs which enables him to attain even higher levels of existence. The self is neither the thinker, as Descartes concluded, nor merely the sum of one's interests and activities, as many philosophers have assumed. The reality is not a self but selfhood. Selfhood is an ongoing process which the individual experiences as a result of his attempting to integrate his biological, psycho-social and spiritual needs.

Dynamic equilibrium implies the process of organic reciprocity whereby the whole affects each part and each part affects the whole. It functions as a compelling drive toward self-integration or individuation in a sense of identity and at-homeness in the world. Organic reciprocity operates in the atom with its electrons and protons, in the molecule with its atoms, in the crystal with its molecules, and throughout the chemical combinations that enter into plant and animal forms. It operates in the solar system and in the vast constellations and galaxies. It functions in man's mental and social life, in his conscious and unconscious as *a sense of responsibility.*

Organicity, or organic reciprocity, operates as the wisdom of nature, of the body and of culture. Organicity gives rise to the processes of self-healing, self-correction and self-equilibration. In organic or living beings such processes proceed from the drive to totality within each part of that totality. Organic reciprocity makes each totality, from the atom to the farthest galaxy, more than the sum of its parts.

The cosmic processes of organicity—whereby totalities act upon each of their parts and its parts upon the totalities—is the source of the Godhood or the superpersonal force in man. Man articulates his ideas of God and experience or organicity through his consciousness of responsibility. That sense of responsibility emanates—not from nature or the cosmos—but from the organic group to which he belongs.

The subpersonal denotes the individual unconscious; the superpersonal the collective unconscious. The human person is the syndrome of needs—biological, psycho-social and spiritual—

and their fulfillment. Freud maintained that the unconscious is dominated by sex needs; Adler stressed psycho-social needs and Jung posited the collective unconscious which is shared by each individual member of the group. The collective unconscious, or superpersonal, is manifest in the drive for creative survival of the organic society. Through chain reaction that drive is rendered co-extensive with the whole of nature or the cosmos. Max Born, a founder of the quantum mechanics and teacher of Oppenheimer, Teller and Fermi, pondered: "The ethical problems which have arisen from the enormous increase in power are even closer to my heart than the scientific and political ones . . . However remote one's work is from technical applications it is a link in the chain of actions and decisions which determine the fate of the human race" (as quoted in review of *My Life and My Views*, in *Commentary*, July 1968).

The superpersonal operates as the culminating and unifying element of all the categories of human existence. It integrates and individuates the personal and the subpersonal. It raises human society above the level of the herd by socializing and humanizing the personal ego. Through dynamic integration the superpersonal drive endows such categories as honesty and responsibility with objective value that transcends the relativism in much of contemporary thought. Honesty implies consistency and coherence, particularly with regard to the symbols in man's universe of values and discourse. Such consistency and coherence satisfy a fundamental human drive for integration which is hampered by untruth. Responsibility pertains to interpersonal activity emanating from the cosmic drive for unity and co-operation among individuals and groups.

What is the scope of unity and cooperation to which responsibility should lead? Through the exercise of freedom in interpersonal and in intergroup relations the individual develops honesty and responsibility as personality traits. Those values motivate the group in its evolvement as an organic community, which accepts responsibility toward its individual and group constituents and to other groups, culminating in ethical nationhood and international cooperation. The process that fosters life, order and growth and that authenticates ethical values as well as meaning and purpose in human existence constitutes nature's God. The Rabbinic maxim "Let all thy deeds be done for the sake of Heaven" (*Avot*, II, 13) calls for the conscious integration of the superpersonal into the personal in all human relations and activities.

Albert Schweitzer defined the underlying religious principle which propelled him toward a spiritually and ethically conducted life as "reverence for life." That insight transformed his entire career. Reverence for life is manifest in an individual's sense of *responsibility* toward the realization of his potentialities and opportunities and in his response to the dangers and challenges of his physical and social environment. The satisfaction of man's spiritual needs requires his integration into a series of concentric areas of responsibility, beginning with life in the home and community and extending to the world.

Although education in the gratification of man's biological and psycho-social requirements is taken for granted, his formal training in satisfying spiritual needs is neglected. Man has profound spiritual need of a sense of responsibility not only for his personal character and conduct but also for his group and national identification. Group religion, which should apply the principles of personal ethics to ethical nationhood, contributes a vital element to the personal equation. When will psychologists and educators incorporate that message into their communications media?

What is the message and mission of group religion? It maintains: (1) that the creative survival of the human species depends upon the group's and nation's responsibility for the character and behavior of their individual adherents; (2) that the motivation for such responsibility, as well as the entire ethos and way of life, is universal and cosmic; and (3) that the education of conscience to support moral behavior under stress and temptation should dominate all education as a lifelong pursuit.

Resistance to equating the study of religion and ethics with secular subjects might be overcome if religious studies were conducted under their original designation, which was *wisdom*. The centrality of God in wisdom can also be taught in a contemporary context. The prophet Jeremiah (16:11) quotes

God as saying that the people of Israel "forsook Him and did not keep His Torah." The Rabbinic interpretation of that text points out that God would not have minded Israel's forsaking Him, were it not that they had failed to keep the Torah. By Torah the Sages understood that which in modern discourse is called ethical nationhood.

If the subject of moral responsibility were to become an integral part of the curricula, the theological aspect could be postponed until there is general acceptance of the naturalistic idea of God. When the God idea is divorced from mythology, anthropomorphism and supernaturalism, Godhood will become identified with all human conduct that strives for the creative survival of the human species in a warless world.

If psychology would recognize group religion as a way of life ministering to the fundamental needs of human nature, it would reckon to a greater extent with the individual's need of involvement in an organic society. The psychologist should be wary of uprooting a patient who may be subject to conflicting interests and loyalties—from his family, religious group or people. Responsibility and loyalty to one's group is essential to mental as well as moral health. If the patient is in conflict with the standards and practices of his group, he should be influenced to correct the group when wrong and keep it on the right path when right. Alienation from one's group leads to a loss of responsible self-identity.

While involvement satisfies the individual's organic need to be a part of a larger totality, he also seeks to be inwardly integrated. Religion has sought unconsciously to achieve such psychic health by demanding wholehearted and whole-souled commitment to God. To love responsibility is to love God. Only through loving one's neighbor does one come to love God. Psychology may learn from religion that through commitment the individual is liberated from his isolation by reckoning with the demands of the superego. Commitment is a prerequisite to mental health and to happiness. Reckoning with does not imply obeying the demands of the superego; it may also involve criticism. Danger lies in *ignoring* the superego.

Religion should not exaggerate group unity and solidarity at the expense of the individuality of the human person. It has intuitively, though gropingly, sought to provide an outlet for the superpersonal drive for organicity, which is as much a process of individuation or selfhood as it is a process of unification. *The moral freedom of the person is the source of responsibility for furthering the organicity of mankind.*

Organic society has evolved the personal process or ego in the individual. When that process functions voluntarily in the form of the superego or conscience, it becomes creative and enlarges the scope of human living. Group religion helps man to mature and attain higher levels of being. It regards the individual as an end in himself, not as a commodity which is expendable. By holding out or denying rewards and by the exercise of sanctions far beyond the power of any human agency, group religion brings the cosmic awareness, or the awareness of Godhood, to the conscious experience of the individual. The religious, as contrasted with the philosophic, belief in the hereafter stressed conservation, not loss, of individuality. It was philosophy, not religion, that conceived immortality as the absorption of the cultivated human intellect in God as the Active Intellect. If the psychiatrist is to be physician to the soul, he must recognize his patient's need of synthesis of freedom and responsibility.

2. WHAT RELIGION CAN LEARN FROM PSYCHOLOGY

Why does man fail to observe the precepts of the religions he professes? The drastic discontinuity between morality and piety is generally assumed to be normal. Not all who pray in public can be trusted in private. The practice of authentic religion has been vitiated by the neurotic functioning of man's ego. It is difficult for the psychologically abnormal to be religiously stable. Many of the traditional beliefs and practices which have persisted in the liturgy of historical religions are irrelevant and have lost their rationale in the light of man's mature wisdom.

George W. Ball wrote:

It is to mankind's eternal embarrassment that human institutions have never kept pace with human requirements. Today, however, the gap which separates the two is large, ominous, and ever widening; for at a time when old political forms are crumbling there has also been a quantum jump in the rate of change. Instead of a rational mold to contain and give meaning to the new wants and capacities of an evolving human society, there have been voids and vacuums as the old political containers crack and decay [*The Discipline of Power*, p. 7].

Before religion can humanize man, man must humanize religion. He must conquer his fear of applying the standards of wisdom, reason, intelligence and love to religion. Man cannot do without religion, but he must transpose it into a new key. The humanization of religion must proceed on two levels—social and personal. Because of their reciprocal relationship, the aberrations on the social level produce aberrations on the personal. Of the various repressed longings, such as narcissism, womb fantasy, mother fixation and father fixation, the last is the source of the *authoritative* character of religion.

Religion as a social phenomenon has always reinforced the authority of those in power. "Power," wrote Bertrand Russell, "is basic to the understanding of the social life and history of man in the same sense in which energy is the fundamental concept of physics. Like energy, power has many forms, such as wealth, armaments, civil authority, influence on opinion . . . Power, like energy, must be regarded as continually passing from any one of its forms into any other, and it should be the business of social science to seek the laws of such transformations" (*Power*, p. 12).

The understanding of power in its various forms elucidates the social aspects of religion. It affords insight into the socio-psychological forces which move persons with a capacity for leadership to assert the will-to-power. Among the species of animals that move in herds, packs, flocks, shoals, and so on, the strongest or swiftest become leaders of their species. In animal life the will-to-power is instinctive and limited to the will-to-live which the leader defends and shares with the rest of his subhuman species. In man the will-to-power becomes part of his ego and is augmented by it.

Limited by his experience, ancient man regarded the gods as the source which conferred upon his leaders the power to command and minister to his needs. If such leaders were not god-chosen, they were deemed gods themselves or descendants of gods. Such was the exalted status of ancient Egyptian Pharaohs, Roman Emperors and, until recently, the Japanese Mikados. Often the gods accompanied the grant of power with a code of laws, as in ancient Babylon, Greece and Rome. According to tradition, YHWH gave the Decalogue to the entire people of Israel but He granted an extraordinary measure of wisdom to King Solomon.

The correlate of the urge to power is the urge to submission, which also has its unconscious and conscious aspects. In the conscious the urge to submission is reinforced by the security-seeking ego. By submission to those who command, the timid, inept and insecure whet the appetite of the élite for even more power. Hence both the governing and the governed abet the *authoritarian* character of religion on a social and superpersonal level.

Authoritarian religion cannot suffer doubt or cynicism concerning the beliefs, myths and wonder-tales with which the naive and untrained mind explains the baffling and awesome events of its experience. Beliefs and myths supply the rationale for ritual observances and taboos as well as moral and legal standards. Deriving their mandate from such supernatural and unassailable sources, the authorities—priestly, military and civil—avoided the appearance of arbitrary rule and defended their domination on grounds of justice, wisdom and love. The resultant inner contradictions which adhered to authoritarian religion in its incipiency still apply. On the one hand, religion asserts the values of wisdom and love to validate authority; on the other, it obstructs the free exercise of reason or intelligence, whose denial drains those values of content. Religion is thus reduced to a way of speaking and praying but not of living.

Authoritarian religion elevates the principle of obedience to the status of a cardinal virtue. Its educational methods ignore all that psychology has taught about reckoning with the spontaneous interests of the child. Though discipline to the point of breaking his will has given way to a more subtle style of brainwashing, the subject matter is presented with the view of inculcating credulity and docility. The subjects of such authoritarian religious education often become victims of neurosis when they have to adjust to the secular environment of freedom. The conflict between their repressed doubts and questionings and the prevailing usage of scientific inquiry has motivated contemporary antagonism and indifference to institutional religion.

Authoritarian religion has left a long trail of blood and tears in its wake. It is doubtful whether even poverty or war has brought greater misery. When James Branch Cabell's *Jurgen* visited hell, he noted that its greatest lake was filled with the blood of warriors for the "Prince of Peace." If authoritarian religion demonstrates less bigotry and sadism than its formal teachings would sanction, the amelioration testifies to the humanity of its adherents rather than its tenets.

At its best, authoritarian religion impedes the full development of the human person by inhibiting his reason or intelligence. The Garden of Eden legend stigmatizes adulthood and self-reliance as the source of sin and suffering. In the dominant Christian tradition man had to be redeemed from "original sin" through the crucifixion of Jesus and faith in his messianic mission. This and other beliefs of authoritarian religions throughout the world still inhibit the development of the overwhelming majority of mankind.

The immaturity of a group religion is reflected in the following attitudes on the part of its adherents:

An attitude of credulity which renders the mind susceptible to irrational and superstitious beliefs in luck, fate or sinister consequences. The superstition that sickness is a punishment for sin persists among neo-orthodox theologians who regard neurosis or mind-sickness as the ultimate chastisement for wrongdoing. Since neuroses are universal, it follows that all men are sinners in a secret and shameful sense. Such childlike suggestibility should give place, with age and education, to the critical faculty and mental independence. Docility toward the dogmas of one's own religion and hostility, on principle, toward those of other religions are symptoms of neurosis.

The belief that salvation is the exclusive prerogative of one's own religion. Its adherents therefore constitute God's Chosen People; and its doctrine becomes *Nihil salus extra ecclesiam.*

Intellectual fixation on some past stage in the history of one's religion as one of divine revelation, and the nostalgic hope for a return to that period.

Inability to think of God in any but anthropomorphic or anthropopathic terms. To the immature mind anything that bears a name is conceived of as a space-occupying entity or person. To the average Christian mind God becomes credible through incarnation, to the average Jewish mind through the theophany at Mount Sinai.

Inability to identify divinity with the natural processes of body or mind. Only faith or spiritual healing meet the specifications of Divinity. God is not discerned in human relations with all their potentialities for good and evil. Truth, justice, love are regarded as *commanded* by God rather than natural manifestations of His presence.

Belief in divine reward and punishment not only for social sins but also for ritual transgressions and unbelief. At a time when *human* reprisals are regarded as mitigated forms of bribery or revenge, *divine* retribution is a savage anachronism. Such doctrine, which justifies the eternal torture of unbaptized children, reflects sadomasochistic efforts on the part of the immature ego to master corresponding impulses of the unconscious.

Otherworldliness or the assumption that man cannot possibly achieve his destiny in this world. This corollary of the belief in reward and punishment attempts to rationalize withdrawal and detachment from the concerns of this world. It acts as an opiate to relieve the true believer of withdrawal guilt symptoms.

The dichotomy of body and soul as a rationale for asceticism which is pleasing to God. Closely related to otherworldiness, asceticism posits the conscious suppression of biological and, especially, sexual impulses. Its advocates exemplify a highly suggestive and infantile self-centeredness accompanied by maso-chistic and immature submissiveness to the superego or censorious conscience.

Abnormal mysticism which is a perversion of normal mysticism. The normal consciousness of the vastness and wonder of the world and of the gap between man's reach and his grasp, or between potential and attainment, finds expression in a sense of identity between the human person and the universal process of organicity or God. Abnormal mysticism, in its various forms, tends to circumvent the communion between the human person and God by eliminating the long and intricate natural steps to arrive at the feeling of oneness.

Psychological insights and experience can foster the continued growth of mature religion by doing what comes naturally: namely, to encourage the untrammeled functioning of reason, intelligence and love.

3.   THE HUMAN PERSON

The will-to-live functions in every living organism as an integrating tendency to maintain its individuality and character. In man this tendency is transformed into the goal of personality involving an awareness of selfhood or self-identity. Man is so constituted that only such awareness can give meaning and consistent direction to his life and yield him deep and abiding satisfaction.

Becoming a human person is made possible through the process of remembering, abstracting, reconstructing experience and envisaging potential situations and forms of self-expression within those situations. Through all these processes there runs a sense of continuity and identity. In any given situation requiring adjustment between that sense of continuity and identity on the one hand and negating or threatening on the other, there arises an intensified awareness or self-consciousness. Self-consciousness has been described by William Stern as both a system of conflict and a means of overcoming it. Its twofold function exemplifies the trait of personality as it unfolds through life in action and its choice of goals. All human life involves a continuous overcoming of obstacles and difficulties. In Stern's analysis the person is

> a living whole, individual, unique, striving toward goals, self-contained and yet open to the world around him . . . The individual must become alienated from the self-evidentness of his merely biological nature, and thereby try to raise himself and the world to the plane of objectivity, and he is constantly dominated by the striving to transcend this alienation on the still higher level of life charged with value in a world of values [*General Psychology*, pp. 71, 83].

Personality or selfhood is a product of interaction between the bodily forces and the environment, both natural and social. Although personality has no locus, its function and continuance are inseparable from the environment. It is experienced as a sense of responsibility for what one thinks, feels or does. The essence of personality is to transcend itself. Through that transpersonal reference the human being enters into cooperation and mutual understanding with his fellows. The more meaningfully he enters into cooperative relations the richer his personality. *There is no limit to the outreach of personality; it extends to mankind as a whole*. To stop at any point short of this all-embracing goal is, at best, a higher form of egoism and bound to end in frustration. Limited loyalties are the correlates of absolute sovereignties.

To deny the fact of personality is to deny the reality of life. Although man transcends mechanistic and scientific law, some would reduce life and mental events to pure mechanism and scientific formulae. Transcendence does not imply overstepping the limits of natural law. It merely implies taking into account a dimension within human nature which some scientists ignore. That is the dimension of value which differentiates human nature from subhuman nature. Value is a manifestation of self-consciousness. Mechanical science, which would reduce human beings to the status of complex objects, ignores the unpredictable impact of personality upon the material world. *Living beings add up to more than the sum of their parts*. Personality is also indivisible; it operates as a totality, each part of which affects the whole through sensory experience. By *conscious* striving to develop his latent talents the human being achieves that *differentia* which determines his essential nature in contrast to the essential nature of other living creatures.

The human experience of selfhood manifests itself as a sense of responsibility for what one thinks, feels or does; a sense of responsibility is experienced emotionally as an imperative call for expression and action. If a person suppresses emotion—holding anger in, loving without showing it, reacting to all situations with a surface calm—he is psychologically sick and incapable of experiencing a sense of responsibility. Personality is thus experienced emotionally as self-identity or responsibility. Insofar as it has direct bearing on man's striving for salvation or self-fulfillment, personality is generally referred to as *soul*. Traditional writers of the past who viewed reality from the standpoint of salvation spoke of soul, not personality. Hence we must reckon with the challenge to the concept of personality implied in that of soul.

Belief in the existence of the soul may have been inferred from dreams. It was conceived as the life energy residing in the blood, breath or the individual's name. Many philosophers represented the soul as the antithesis of body. Plotinus, Plato and, to a lesser degree, Descartes contributed largely to the theory of dualism which for centuries dominated both philosophy and theology in the Western world.

Some modern psychologists extended denial of the existence of the soul to rejection of the reality of the human person. Their error in disallowing the hypothesis of soul was preceded by that of Laplace, who renounced the hypothesis of God. When a belief, despite changes of form, persists, it incorporates authenticity in human experience and expresses vital aspirations. Both experience and hope reflect some underlying reality. Through their perennial belief in the human soul, men have testified that *there is more to the human being than meets the eye;* they have averred *that every human being should so live as to bring that hidden treasure to the surface.* This experience and hope are implied in every one of the ancient conceptions of the soul, from the primitive to the philosophic, from belief in the ghost-double to the notion of some immortal essence.

Man's awareness of his own soul confirms the intuition concerning his creativity and potential. No description of his powers or achievements and no definition of his being can exhaust all that is to him and in him. Thanks to this unmeasured fund of potentiality man is not a fixed quantity or quality. He is incalculable and unpredictable; above all, he is creative. Potentiality is reality waiting to be realized.

The soul is the creative plus in human nature, as God is the creative plus of nature as a whole. God represents the inexhaustible fund of creative potentiality in nature by virtue of which it transcends the mechanical. This parallelism between God and the soul is recognized in traditional religion which defines man as "created in the image of God," and in the words of the Psalmist: "Thou hast made him little less than divine." Awareness of man's soul affirms the worth of man, as the knowledge of God confirms the infinite worth of nature as a whole. The Jewish mystic who spoke of the soul as a "portion of the God above" anticipated the poet and Spinoza who defined man as a bit of God himself. Neither the human plus (soul) nor the cosmic plus (God) can be exhaustively described. In their case, definitions consist in negating inadequate description—in other words, *negative theology*.

Man is a conglomerate of sensate experience and emotional drives which give rise to his sense of values. Values which constitute wisdom enter the ego-consciousness through the social mediation of the superego. Failure to heed the voice of the superego or conscience effaces the distinction between man and beast. Well-being is nature's way of impelling both man and animal to perpetuate the species and to self-realization. The superperson or superego seeks to prevent the sex drive from functioning as an end in itself in total disregard of social consequences. It likewise directs the will to competence or power into socially constructive channels. Through restraint and moderation, justice and kindness, the superego combats greed and preemptive aggression.

To the extent that the human being possesses soul or personality—which contemporary existentialists refer to as sense of identity—it impels man to cooperate with his fellowman. Thus that polarity of everything in nature, which, by functioning as responsibility in all human relations, prompts men and nations to self-affirmation and to cooperation. The control and direction of the conscious desire for well-being and competence as ends in themselves derive from man's inherent sense of responsibility and his desire to cooperate with his fellowmen. That spiritual dimension operates, for the most part, superconsciously, in the interests of human life as a whole, through the medium of the organic society to which the individual belongs. Many suffer neurosis because of their insensibility to the demands of the *superpersonal sense of responsibility*. Nature's God demands that man act in a spirit of responsibility for the general good. Psychoanalysis should help the patient become aware of the superconscious or the spiritual dimension of his personality. He should learn to transcend his instinctive drives and adopt new goals of responsible and social action.

In his striving for self-fulfillment the individual yearns for self-possession or self-mastery. Self-discipline reinforced by specific rules of conduct and laws may be likened to the insistent ringing of an alarm clock. The attraction of monastic orders for some is their enforcement of rigid rules of self-discipline. Ascetics who indulge in self-flagellation pay a price for the sake of self-mastery. Although such extreme exercises may degenerate into spiritual pride, respect for law and self-discipline reflecting a free and autonomous sense of moral responsibility should not be deprecated.

The interplay of self-expression and self-mastery molds the kind of personality which Aristotle ascribes to the good man (*spoudaios*):

> The good man is of one mind with himself, and desires the same things with all his soul (i.e. with every part of his nature), and wishes for himself that which both is and seems good, and seeks it by action (for it is a mark of a good man to exert himself actively for the good). To the good man existence is good . . . Such a man also wishes to live with himself; for his own company is pleasant to him. The memory of his past life is sweet, and for his future he

has good hopes; and such hopes are pleasant. His mind, moreover, is stored with matter for contemplation . . . The same things give him pleasure and pain at all times and not different things at different times, since he is not apt to change his mind [*Ethics*, X, 4].

Men and women of superior intelligence, creative ability and ethical character yearn to develop their potentialities for the general good as well as for self-actualization. The vague and superconscious hunger for a higher and better form of life functions consciously among the spiritually gifted. Their lives testify to the reality of Godhood. For Godhood is that polarity which directs the interplay of individuality and interactivity in man. Insofar as universal reciprocity controls bodily and social desires and directs them toward self-fulfillment it functions as God.

A prerequisite to knowing God as the Power that makes for human self-fulfillment or happiness is the faith that human nature is capable of achieving it. To believe in God we have to exercise wisdom; to believe in man we have to exercise faith. If despite the prevalence of corruption and cruelty we can discern some evidence of a spiritual order, we are likely to *know* God. But before we seek such evidence in others we must discover it in ourselves. It has been said that there can be revealed *to* us only that which is revealed *in* us. Accordingly, the first step in achieving a knowledge of God is to know oneself.

The knowledge of one's own person is not only a *prerequisite to the knowledge of God;* it also partakes of the very knowledge of God. One must identify a principle of life which derives not only from one's biological and social needs but from nature as a whole. In the yearning for salvation or happiness, for truth, loyalty, justice, freedom and peace, man experiences something of which he is generally unconscious, *not because it is subconscious, but because it is superconscious.* Anyone who becomes aware of that superconscious yearning in himself cannot be so vain as to believe that he is unique. The most difficult step in achieving a knowledge of God is that of knowing oneself.

The interpretation of the cosmos depends upon the interpretation of the human person. Without the striving for inner unity and growth which constitute personality, man cannot discover unity and growth in the world about him. A philosophy of history involves the projection of the sense of inner unity, memory and anticipation upon a network of social relationships. The experiences of others, remote in space and time, become our own, extending the horizon of our own being. While sharing in the events of our contemporaries we relive the experiences of our ancestors and influence the lives of our descendants. That enhancement is originative and creative; it envisages the full realization of man's spiritual potential.

Pre-modern theologians assumed that salvation required self-identification or union with God through the transcendence of sin and mortality. With the elimination by death of the physical aspects of man, he was deemed fit to assume the godly attribute of immortality. In modern psychological terms, immortality might be transmuted into the assumption that man's spiritual dimension or moral responsibility lives on through an endless chain of creative consequences. Those consequences constitute immortality for the person and society.

CHAPTER V

Man's Sense of Destiny

WHEN Nicholas Copernicus (1473–1543) disproved the Ptolemaic theory that the earth was the center of the universe, he unbound the chains which had shackled scientific theory and observation for close to two millennia. Two hundred years after that Copernican revolution, Isaac Newton conceived "the gigantic hypothesis that the motion of the heavenly bodies and the motion of ordinary bodies on earth are of essentially the same kind. By means of this insight, formulated in his theory of gravitation, he was able to explain the theories of Copernicus, Galileo and Kepler" (John Herman Randall, Jr., and Justus Buchler, *Philosophy, An Introduction*, p. 71). Along with their rejection of an earth- and man-centered universe, the scientists of the late sixteenth, seventeenth and eighteenth centuries undermined the classical and traditional concepts of man's destiny.

How did theologians and philosophers shore up the weakened foundations of man's moral and spiritual life? Thomistic theology—the attempted synthesis of Aristotelian logic and supernaturalist church doctrine by St. Thomas Aquinas and other thirteen-century schoolmen—was discredited. Mathematical science, which followed the decline of scholasticism, used the rationalistic deductive method to explore scientific theories. In his application of the mathematical method, Baruch Spinoza (1632–1677) formulated his system of ethics *more geometrico*

and laid the groundwork for modern naturalism by his conception of nature and man's place in it.

Spinoza, a rigid determinist, rejected the traditional idea of
man's freedom of will. His concept of God excluded the
traditional attribute of providence as well as belief in miracles.
He retained and emphasized the traditional ethical values by
categorizing them in terms of metaphysical "necessity." The
principal function of knowledge or reason was, according to
Spinoza, to enable man to bring his passions under control:
"The divine law which renders mankind truly happy and
teaches the perfect way of life is of universal application
and common to all; indeed we have so deduced it from the
nature of man and shown it to be innate, written as it were
in his heart and his mind" (*Theol.*, V, 100).

*Spinoza's deduction that the knowledge of the divine law
derives from the knowledge of the nature of man, instead of
the reverse as assumed in the religious tradition, gives us the
first glimpse of religion in a new key.* That divine law is the
mathematically structured order of the universe, which is discovered by the human mind. By accepting that law and living
it man may achieve true freedom or salvation. "He who desires
to govern his emotions and appetites from a love of liberty
alone should strive all he can to know virtues and their causes,
and to fill his mind with that joy which springs from a true
knowledge of them" ("On Human Freedom," *Ethics*, Pt. V, prop.
IV). Habituation in the practice of seeking out the causal order
of one's emotions leads to a grasp of predeterminate law, as it
pervades the cosmos. The resultant sense of fulfillment Spinoza
characterizes as "the intellectual love of God."

Spinoza's philosophy of salvation could not displace the
Judeo-Christian concepts which had served the Western world
for centuries. It was based on a paradoxical concept of freedom
which negates the very essence of moral responsibility. If the
capacity to choose among alternative courses of action is an
illusion, then all striving for salvation becomes meaningless.
That striving derives from the idea of a future and of a purpose
to be freely striven for. Spinoza's conceptions of illusory freedom
and of the intellectual love of God are irrelevant for the average

person who is no intellectual recluse and whose life situation poses constant choice among baffling practical and moral alternatives. Nor could Spinoza's contemplative views relate to the activist drive for self-fulfillment as new opportunities were opened up by the experimental sciences and modern technology.

The intellectual revolution which refuted the anthropocentric idea of the universe extended man's physical, economic and political horizons to encompass the goal of human betterment. During the sixteenth and seventeenth centuries works such as Thomas More's *Utopia*, Campanella's *State of the Sun* and Bacon's *New Atlantis* proffered idealist, if not idyllic, solutions to the problems of human nature and destiny. Abandoning his reliance on faith, works and repentance, man examined the physical and social conditions under which he lived. There was a demand for political action to improve the social order, by removing long-standing injustices and by encouraging the process of individual growth and self-fulfillment. The great intellectual and political upheaval of the eighteenth century gave rise to the assumption that man was on the march toward a brighter and happier future. There was nothing better for the individual than to keep in step with that march. Therein lay his destiny.

Having repudiated the theological notion that man was intrinsically depraved and could be saved only through the divine grace mediated by the Church, some eighteenth-century thinkers analyzed human nature in terms of environmental and educational factors. They sought solutions in political revolution and in educational reform. But the age-old habit of looking to the individual himself as the deciding factor in the improvement of his life was too strong to be abandoned. The power of reason was supposed to order his experience into a pattern most compatible with the well-being both of the individual and of society.

The two conceptions of human nature which had always prevailed became particularly dominant during those years. According to Hobbes, man is naturally egoistic; but under the influence of sympathy his egoism undergoes the development whereby the relation of one's own well-being to that of others is so clearly apprehended that to care for others becomes part of one's very egoism. Egoism is then termed "enlightened."

Due to the divinely established harmony of the cosmos, man's selfish aims, particularly as they tend to become enlightened, providentially lead to the general good. According to Bishop Butler (1692–1752), human nature is inherently so constituted as to be simultaneously impelled by self-interests and by altruistic interests. "There are as real indications in human nature," says Butler (*Sermons*, Preface to Sermon I, II), "that we are made for society and to do good to our fellow creature, as that we are intended to take care of our own life and private good."

One of the most revolutionary notions advanced during the Age of Enlightenment was that all men are born equal. *Thus if man's political, economic and social institutions were based on the laws inherent in his nature the millennium would be achieved.* In his *Histoire Naturelle* (1794) Buffon, one of the Encyclopedists, hailed "man [as] the culmination of the process of nature. Man is the revolutionary, changing the surface of the earth, uniting with his fellows to subdue nature and bend her processes to his purposes" (John Herman Randall, Jr., *The Making of the Modern Mind*, p. 455).

Challenging these views Rousseau declared that "natural" was the antithesis of "rational." Man acts naturally when he yields to his feelings and is not restrained by reason as embodied in custom and tradition. Man is naturally good; the social institutions alone have corrupted him. Change them and he will realize his innate goodness. To become fully human, man should cultivate those of his feelings which find expression in good will. The human differential is his capacity to exercise intelligence.

Thus the Romanticists "reasoned" themselves back into the camp of the traditionalists who, though subscribing to the theological dogma of original sin and human depravity, affirmed with equal ardor man's original state of perfection. The dogma of human depravity played into the hands of the Romanticists who attributed individual depravity to corrupt government and institutionalized religion.

The conception of human nature as fundamentally a matter of habituation served as a "rationale" for a return to the past. The feeling of piety, which leads one to cling to long-standing customs and routine, often takes precedence over objective reasoning. That retreat from reason can be noted among the intellectuals by the end of the eighteenth century. Among the masses, whose life was being transformed by the industrial revolution, evangelistic revivalism revitalized the traditional view of man based on the doctrine of original sin. (In Protestant countries the force of that revivalism is still far from spent. The lengths to which Protestantism carried its war against rationalism and in behalf of blind acceptance of traditional supernaturalism have evoked strong antipathy, particularly on the European continent, against religion and all its works.)

Kant, Goethe and Hegel made significant contributions to the concept of the uniqueness of the individual personality. Influenced by Hume's empirical skepticism and Rousseau's negation of medieval rationalism, Kant demonstrated that notions of a cosmos, of God and of soul are regulative ideas built, as it were, into the human mind. Thus while man cannot know reality in itself, he can experience that part of reality which is the creation of his mind.

Kant envisaged man not as a kind of biological entity with a soul, but as a being whose uniqueness was implicit in his capacity for self-directed growth. Man can only be known through practical reason with its ideas of God, freedom and immortality. Such ideas derive neither from the speculative nor from the empirical approach to reality but from the assumption that man is a moral or responsible being. His essential nature demands that he live a life of virtue in which his affections and desires collaborate with his sense of duty so that he would *want* most to do what he *ought* to do. For the spiritual man it is natural to suppress the lower desires and to follow the autonomous call of duty.

In *Faust*, Part II, Goethe sets forth in highly dramatic fashion a new idea of man as process. His Faust becomes fully human not through his vast range of experiences and suffering but by what he does to achieve his destiny. Thus Goethe synthesized two distinct tendencies: the traditional outlook of effecting man's self-improvement through his inner attitudes, habits and ideas, and the modern tendency of looking to social, political and educational reform for improvement in the external conditions of his life.

This synthesis was formulated by Hegel in his *Phenomenology of Mind*. It opens up new vistas for the understanding of the relation of man to his environment. Hegel counters the scientific, and common-sense, view of things which treats them as existing per se and whose essence is independent of the human mind. He maintains that whatever we know about things—whether due to common-sense perception of them or to scientific grasp of the permanent elements in them—is a mental construct and part of the universe of discourse. Hence that outer world which is scientifically viewed as determining the inner man is not something alien and objective with a dead objectivity. It is, in a sense, just as much a product of the mind as is whatever man does with his will, his thoughts and his emotions. To the extent that reason pervades his inner life, it also pervades his outer life. The two are one, and reason, truth or absolute meaning is in the one as well as in the other.

In addition to this conception of the relation of man to his environment, Hegel's contribution to the conception of reality is a return with deepened understanding to the Heraclitian (*circa* 500 B.C.E.) thesis that reality is not a static entity but an ongoing process. Hegel, however, did not accept the traditional contrast of Being and Becoming. To him Being is Becoming. "It should be enunciated," he says, "that all things are contradictory in themselves" (*The Science of Logic*, I, 47). Hence reason or absolute meaning of reality is to be sought in dynamic, not in static, universals. Universals must be so formulated as to indicate that aspect of things which emphasizes their straining to transcend the condition in which they happen to be. That straining, or *nisus*, is their dialectic.

Hegel regarded man not as a self-contained individual to be improved through inferences from abstract thinking about the self, but as a cell in a social organism. Resort must be had to that instrument whereby reason, which is within man in man's world, comes to light. Since the State brings human beings into close association in all those activities through which they find fulfillment, it is therefore the one indispensable instrument of man's salvation.

Shortly after the religio-philosophic trend had reached its apogee in the idealistic philosophies of the early decades of the nineteenth century, it suffered a cataclysmic shock from the impact of successive and spectacular scientific discoveries. The exalted idea that man had of himself as the purpose of creation, as little lower than the angels and as the special object of divine solicitude gave way first to Charles Darwin's discovery of man's evolution from subhuman species as a result of the process of natural selection. About the same time, Karl Marx expounded the determining role of economic production in political and social power and Sigmund Freud proved that man's conscious life masks a complex of impulses which lie hidden in the dark caverns of the unconscious. Hence all moral and spiritual postures were disguises for inner animal compulsions. Religion was an illusion and civilization a disease.

The present state of mind with regard to the meaning or value of human life was summed up by Elmer Rice:

> We have taken the human mechanism apart in an effort to find out why it does not tick, but we have not yet discovered the formula for reassembling it so that its triumphant carillon may ring out to heaven. In splitting the atom and splitting the ego, we have unleashed forces that may destroy us, unless we find a synthesis that will employ atomic energy for peaceful uses, and psychic energy for restoring to man a belief in his own dignity and creative potentialities [*Saturday Review*, December 17, 1955].

Far from solving the problem of human destiny, that statement bespeaks a formula for assembling the scientifically dismembered human being and providing the synthesis which he needs to achieve verifiable faith in himself and awareness of nature's God. From there experts in the human sciences should collaborate in the study of man to help him avoid frustration and achieve fulfillment.

The biological sciences have demonstrated man's kinship with subhuman species. The social sciences have revealed the primitive passions which motivate human conduct. Their conclusions, all pointing to man's imperfect humanity and unrealized potentialities, define the fundamental challenge to religion and ethics. Although many modern spiritual leaders are aware of the need to effect a radical transformation in the nature of man, their religious institutions throughout the ages have been so involved in and vitiated by fanaticism and conflict that they themselves now require a radical overhauling.

If the historical religions have not satisfied the spiritual hunger of their communicants, it is because of the institutional moral lag between profession and performance. Taking the church to task for condoning "the remnant of the pattern of slavery," Reinhold Niebuhr wrote:

> The Christian Church did not seriously challenge these customs. The political community proved itself more rigorous than the Christian community in guarding the dignity of man. The Church, as our Negro friends constantly remind us, was the most rigorously segregated institution in the nation. That segregation wittingly or unwittingly gave a religious aura to racial prejudice ["Proposal to Billy Graham" in *Christian Century*, August 8, 1956].

The failure of group religion to cultivate ethical values and its concentration on piety and polity have rendered both church and synagogue irrelevant to the moralization of human character and to the betterment of human relations. The fundamentalist and supernaturalist approach in traditional religions is at variance with emphasis on ethics and responsibility. Although there is a growing trend among the communicants of churches and synagogues to regard their traditional beliefs and practices as symbolic of ethical and psycho-social values, that reinterpretation has been haphazard and limited for the most part to the columns of progessive religious publications and the iconoclastic advocates of secular theology.

If those beliefs and practices are to be relevant to contemporary needs of the human spirit, they must be reinterpreted in the light of understandable and communicable experience, which does not hide behind clouds of mystifying paradoxes.

Even paradox, to be acceptable, must be identified as universal experience and not claimed to be private mystery. The thought pattern by which we might revitalize traditional religion must be based upon an empirical and verifiable version of religion as universally experienced. Such a thought pattern would identify, from the standpoint of human progress and perfectibility, what is common to all religions, ancient and modern, primitive and highly developed. *It would view each religion as a way of life which is shared by a group that accepts some common goal as salvation. Its function is, therefore, to prescribe for its adherents what they must do and believe in relation to the Power upon which they depend for their salvation.*

This statement implies, in the first place, that religion exists as *religions* through which their adherents are aware of themselves as a people, church or organic fellowship. This does not prevent any individual from isolating himself from his group and living out his religion by himself. Most religious ascetics have done this. If, however, in his self-imposed isolationism the individual works out an original way of life, it becomes a social religion only when he returns to his people, who then adopt that way of life. Otherwise his very religion is the embodiment of irresponsibility.

Second, that humanist conception would revolutionize the attitude toward religion. Instead of assuming God as the determining factor in religion, man must derive the idea of God from responsibility which is indispensable to his creative survival. As the indispensable means to salvation, Godhood redeems man from the effects of his irresponsibility. *Since every one of the historical religions is in a state of crisis, they must be doing something wrong. If they were to teach ethical nationhood as the means of salvation,* they would revolutionize the general attitude toward religion. When man's spiritual values enhance his personality as an individual and his creative contributions to society, he will have attained a full measure of humanity and God-likeness.

Man is still far removed from the goal of salvation. Unlike other living creatures he must take a hand in his own metamorphosis. He must consciously and deliberately share in the cosmic or divine process which impels him to become fully human. Although he owes both life itself and the drives to make the best use of it to a Power that is transcendent and divine, he must use his own creative energies to cooperate with that Power for his own development. *Man must treat his life as a work of art.* As a work of art, the life we must try to live has a logic of its own, a logic compounded of will, skill, reason, intelligence and love. Utilizing that logic, we could develop a pattern of values which would help us weld our desires and our duties, our opportunities and our purposes, into a harmonious whole. Such a pattern of life would enable us to organize our lives rationally, spiritually and creatively.

If religion is to become a vital force in human life, it must be dissociated from magic and theurgy and be made coextensive with man's effort to better his own nature and nation. To effect a Copernican revolution in traditional religions man must view the achievement of human destiny as the *premise* from which he can arrive at a tenable conception of God. By proceeding from man the knowable to God the unknown, he may understand what God means to him through his increasing knowledge of self.

This new development in group religion is part of the general tendency to replace faith in tradition and blind obedience to authority with an awareness of life's authentic values. It conceives religion as a means of rendering man creative and responsible. Group religion can save man from the danger of being robotized by technology, of being subjected to dictatorship or to the anonymous authority of the human crowd.

This new development in group religion marks the latest stage in the evolution of man. To achieve salvation man must synthesize his selfhood and otherhood, the two human aspects of that polarity which mark all existence and thought. *The capacity to play a conscious role in his own evolution is man's prerogative.* Such creative freedom fulfills the Judeo-Christian doctrine that man was made in the image of God. As the artist of his own life his values should be multi-dimensional—encompassing wisdom, reason, intelligence and love. Man's artistry inheres in the depth and consistency of his commitment to those values.

The art of living requires the interaction of a harmonious personality and a cooperative society. Group religion should help man to play a conscious role in his own evolution, to elect self-metamorphosis as his destiny.

Self-metamorphosis is man's vocation. To the extent that he engages in that vocation, he lives the good and full life. To the extent that he ignores or neglects it, he contributes to mankind's doom. "Man is born to become human," wrote Karl Jaspers, "not to perish as an unsuccessful experiment" (*The Future of Mankind*, p. 230).

The nature of man, far from being a finished affair, is still in the making. Just as modern man is an improvement over the caveman, so his continued development may be assumed in the process of emergent evolution. Metamorphosis occurs on a psycho-social as well as a biological level. "Mankind," according to Jung, "is still in the main in a psychological state of infancy— a level which cannot be leaped over" ("Two Essays on Analytical Psychology" *Beziehungen*, pp. 203 ff).

The three aspects of human nature—biological, psycho-social and spiritual—must be coordinated if man is to undergo a meaningful metamorphosis in his relations to his fellowmen. The ethical function of religion will be achieved when men realize that wisdom, justice and love can replace the dominance of brute force and cunning and that human differences are neither so deep nor so irreconcilable that they cannot be bridged by compromise. Only then will men finally eliminate fear, anxiety, aggressiveness and licentiousness from their inner being.

The transformation that has taken place in man from his beginnings as a cave dweller to the present day points to a metamorphosis in his relations to his fellowmen in a direction away from brute force and cunning under their manifold guises. "Moral progress," writes Bertrand Russell, "has been occurring throughout recorded history. We no longer sell our parents to neighboring cannibals when they become too old for work. We do not indulge in hecatombs of human sacrifice as the Aztecs did. British of the present day are horrified by the penalty of being hanged, drawn and quartered, which was cheerfully inflicted not so very long ago" (*Saturday Review*, December 21, 1957).

The process of human metamorphosis has been subject to acceleration. When we reflect upon what has happened to Western mankind during so relatively short a period as the last four or five centuries, we cannot but conclude that man as a type is undergoing transformation in his inner and outer life. The manifold increase in population, the lengthening of man's life-span, the improvement in his health, the extended influence of the masses, the enrichment of their mental content, the widening of their life horizon and above all, the establishment of large areas where the beginnings of democracy are replacing authoritarianism, these are not mere quantitative changes in man's being. They spell qualitative growth and spiritual maturity. We have traveled far from the generally accepted theory that war is the legitimate *ultima ratio regum*, though still regarded as an inescapable evil.

Erich Fromm writes:

> A hundred years ago it was a widely accepted belief that no one had responsibility for his neighbor. It was assumed, and scientifically proved by economics, that the laws of society made it necessary to have a vast army of poor and jobless people in order to keep the economy going. Today, hardly anybody would dare voice this principle. It is generally accepted that nobody should be excluded from the wealth of the nation, either by the laws of nature or by those of society [*The Sane Society*, p. 335].

Edward Alexander Westermarck in *The Origin and Development of Moral Ideas* came to the conclusion that the altruistic or benevolent tendencies in man have increased and are capable of "indefinite extension." This capacity for indefinite moral and spiritual growth buttresses faith—whether empirical or intuitive —in human decency. Without that faith there can be no authentic idea of God.

It has taken considerable thought, devotion and patience to bring mankind to its present stage of development. Why may not further expenditure of such efforts carry mankind to even higher levels of attainment? Man's latent potentialities are far from exhausted. He may yet eliminate resort to violence and bloodshed in the conflicts of international and other group interests, as have been devised for the resolution of interpersonal differences. "The creation of man's world, according to Plato, consists in the victory of persuasion over force" (Whitehead, *Adventures in Ideas*, p. 105). That indeed may well constitute the key principle of what is involved in having man shed all vestiges of his jungle heredity.

In common with other organisms which function in order to realize their full capacities man may ultimately suppress destructive and divisive forces which have thus far impeded his own and society's creative capacities. In such a society, which is ethical democracy, men would find real fulfillment.

The drive in mankind to outdo and transcend itself is as real and relentless as the drive to self-perpetuation. "Man is the only creature who refuses to be what he is," declares Albert Camus (*The Rebel*). And Alex Hrdlicka bases his belief in the continuing evolution of man on the following reasons:

> The one is that, according to all tests, Man is still as plastic —impressionable and changeable—as he ever was, if not more so; while the second is that Man is developing new and powerful evolutionary factors of his own.

> About the greatest factors of contemporaneous and future progressive human evolution, however, are the thirst and striving for the better, for something even higher and more distinguished in every line . . . The more man is developed intellectually, the more there is of this striving for a higher state, for happiness, progress, and intellectual freedom [Alex Hrdlicka, "The Problem of Human Evolution" in *Science and Man*, pp. 35, 39].

Man must utilize to the full the gift of self-knowledge. Occasionally a thinker or saint caught the meaning of man's endless search for the permanent good or glimpsed the significance of his ethical strivings. Inherent in the sense of sin and despair which darken men's lives is the experience of frustration and failure. The human being who has contributed nothing to society is like the Peer Gynt of Ibsen's play who "never really knew himself." After years of restless self-seeking and licentious satisfaction of his ego-centered appetites, Peer met his end as so much slag on the waste heap, to be melted by the angel of Death into nothing.

Many biologists maintain that the evolutionary process is not confined to the natural adaptation and selection of the species. Using the concept of *emergent evolution*, they discern a biological force that enables certain members of a species to develop deviations which augment their chances of survival. With his increasing self-awareness man, too, may metamorphose himself into a higher type of creature—a creature that participates in the creative process with a growing capacity or freedom to achieve it.

The concept of man's metamorphosis as constituting his destiny is clearly implied in the writings of some of the ancient philosophers and medieval theologians. "How contemptible a thing is man," says Seneca, "unless he can raise himself above humanity" (*Naturales Questiones*, Book 1, Preface 5). Both the philosophers and the theologians sought to translate into terms of the current thinking of their day the deep yearning which the various religions of mankind had voiced—a yearning for the consummation in the hereafter of that essential fulfillment which is denied man in this world. The belief in the world-to-come generally included a conception of man as free from the pain of suffering that marred his happiness in this world, and especially free from the temptations and evil impulses that corrupted his nature. Such a being cannot but be different from man as we know him. Hence the religious traditions, which took post-mortem existence for granted, were unconscious anticipations of the possibility of his metamorphosis.

Although Shaw leaves his Don Juan in Hell he gives that miscreant all the lines: "As long as I can conceive something better than myself, I cannot be easy, unless I am striving to bring it into existence, or clearing the way for it. That is the law of my life. That is the working within me of life's incessant aspiration to higher organization, wider, deeper self-consciousness, and clearer self-understanding" (*Man and Superman*). Though the average person is seldom aware of such a law, and even the exceptional person only when he is most alive, the fact remains that, judged objectively, and seen from a long perspective, man gives the impression of being driven by some inner force to transcend himself.

The limits of potentiality in subhuman beings are transmitted unchanged from generation to generation. The subhuman animal transmits its biological impulses and drives. As long as the environment remains unchanged, that species of animal survives. Man, however, creates civilization, which is new environment—physical, social and cultural. This new environment enlarges the horizons of his potentialities. Suppose man were to avail himself of his knowledge of biology to change his genetic nature or to regulate the growth of population; suppose he became sufficiently expert, psychologically and sociologically, to alter the organization of his cultural and economic life. Can there be any doubt that he would hardly be recognizable by his ancestors as their descendant?

Fundamentally our lives are what we make them. "Man does not merely exist as an organic product," says Lewis Mumford. "He makes something of himself, and the making of man is the meaning of history" (*Conduct of Life*, p. 37). Man's self-consciousness is the principal agency in the process of transforming him from a being dominated by biological drives and instincts into a being progressively conscious of what he is heading for. *The organic totality of the forces which impel and draw us on to transcend ourselves is nature's God, or Godhood.* Even the fatalist dictum does not entirely negate free will: *Discunt fata volentem, nolentem, trahunt* (The fates lead the willing and drag the unwilling). But human responsibility and self-conscious choice predominate in the well-known Rabbinic saying: "Where a man wishes to go, thither he is led" (*Makkot* 10a). Even the Icelandic saying, "Every fate is to be overcome by bearing it," implies a degree of mastery over fate. Together with being a biological survival and a product of circumstance, man is also a fashioner of his own destiny in that he is endowed not only with life but also with creativity. In the biblical story of Creation man is represented as a reflection of Divinity. That fact makes him in part the architect or artist of his own life.

The inner drive to make the most of life emerges into consciousness in moments of illumination which are experienced by people who have attained a certain level of maturity and cultivation. In the context of life in general, as it manifests itself in numerous changing and evolving species, man's relentless will to salvation is the drive to metamorphosis raised to the level of self-awareness. "In discovering himself," writes Julian Huxley, "as the sole or main agent of evolution for securing the possible future advance of life, man is linked with the cosmic process of evolution. He sees himself as united with the rest of living nature, one of innumerable products of its evolution, yet unique in the responsibility and opportunity which he enjoys, of carrying on the process to new levels" ("Evolutionary Humanism" in *Standard*, XXX, 1).

"It is the pent up social feeling in us," says Alfred Adler, "that urges us to reach a higher stage and to rid ourselves of the errors that mark our public life and our personality. This social feeling exists within us and endeavors to carry out its purpose. It is not strong enough to hold its own against all opposing forces. The justified expectation persists that in a far-off age, if mankind is given time enough, the power of social feeling will triumph over all that opposes it. Then it will be as natural to man as breathing. For the present the only alternative is to understand and to reach the conclusion that this will happen" (*Social Interest: A Challenge to Mankind*, p. 35).

Insofar as various religions and philosophies have stressed the difference between what man is and what he ought to be, they have been acting under the pressure of the human drive to self-metamorphosis. It was mainly prejudice against both religion and philosophy that led Karl Marx to accuse them of merely sanctioning the *status quo*, of interpreting the world instead of changing it. The fact is that there has hardly been a scientist or philosopher who has not contributed to human progress. Plato, Aristotle, the Stoics, Thomas Aquinas, Spinoza, Hobbes, Locke and Rousseau have certainly left their impress on the political life of mankind. To prove that religion has enhanced civilization one need only point to the ancient religions as well as to the great historic religions. The good they accomplished may have spent itself, and the good they sought to accomplish may be entirely unsuited for our day. Yet without them mankind would have been far less removed from the beasts of the jungle than it is today.

Both philosophers and theologians have assumed that man's nature, rather than the conditions of life, requires transformation. If their specific teachings are out of tune with the needs of our times, which they could not have anticipated, why not study anew the functioning of the will to self-fulfillment? If the idea of God is not based on the belief in theophanies and miracles, then let it be based on each person's need to be needed and therefore to be involved with some self-discipline and self-perpetuating society. Even Berdyaev, an existentialist theologian, who held to the centrality of the God idea with a profundity and intensity scarcely equaled in modern thinking, admits that "revelation presupposes faith in man and in his higher nature, which renders possible that religious upheaval which we call revelation" (Nicholas Berdyaev, *Spirit and Freedom*, p. 94). The religio-ethical traditions of mankind recognize this relentless and compulsive drive in a man to rise above the limitations of his nature.

In Samuel Alexander's view the mind of man is the prelude to Godhood. Deity is "the next higher empirical quality for any level of existence . . . There is nothing in mind which requires us to stop and say this is the highest empirical quality which time can produce from now throughout the infinite time to come. It is only the highest empirical quality which we who are minds happen to know" (*Time, Space and Deity*, II, 346). He adds that it was legitimate to imagine finite beings which were called angels, because angels are a "pictorial embodiment of the conception forced on us by the fact that there is this series of levels of existence."

Alexander's concept of angels approximates the thesis of this author and of ancient religious writers, namely that man is undergoing metamorphosis. The Jewish Scriptures declared that "there is none so righteous on earth as not to sin" (Eccles. 7:20), and they proved their case in the portrayal of all the Hebrew spiritual heroes, including Moses, as deficient in fulfilling the will of God. At the same time, the Hebrew Bible envisaged the advent of the perfectly righteous man. Said Jeremiah: "Behold the days are coming, says the Lord, when I will raise up for David a righteous branch and he shall reign as King and deal wisely, and shall execute justice and righteousness in the land" (Jer. 23:5–6). The Prophet Isaiah (11:2–5) depicts that King as Messiah who will redeem not only Israel but all mankind.

In line with a later otherworldly outlook on life, that metamorphosis was conceived as taking place in the hereafter or in heaven. That man might activitate his higher potentialities and become as perfect in the present world as he was when he came forth from the hand of God was altogether unthinkable. Jesus is quoted as having said: "At the resurrection, people . . . are like angels of God in heaven" (Matt. 22:30). Both Maimonides and Thomas Aquinas subscribed to the view that man's intellect renders him capable of being assimilated to the Divine Intellect. That consummation, however, can take place only after death. "When it [the soul] is separated from the body," wrote Joseph Albo, "it will, by reason of its obedience to God's will, unite with the permanent thing [the Active Intellect] it apprehended. It will thus attain the rank of angels" (*Ikkarim*, IV, Lauterbach's translation, p. 296). According to the Jewish statesman and theologian Isaac Abravanel, God created the world for the sake of man, who is therefore the highest being in creation. Only in his present condition is man inferior to angels who are nearer to God than he is. Ultimately, by virtue of his possession of free will, man is destined to prove that he is superior to them (*Yeshuot M'shiho* 47a).

Henri Bergson stressed the possibility of man's metamorphosis in this world which derives from his philosophy of "Creative Evolution." He bases his hopes upon the fact that throughout the ages there have arisen persons whom he designated as "mystics." The spiritual quality of creative love which they have radiated will ultimately transform man's moral order and enable man to achieve a higher form of existence. Thomas Mann must have harbored these ideas when he wrote: "There is at bottom only one problem in the world. How does one burst the cocoon and become a butterfly?" (*Dr. Faustus*, Ch. XXX, p. 307).

In his discussion of moral values and justice Edmond Cahn wrote:

> The living generation of men always hold a supreme cos-
> mopolastic *opportunity*. Though they may blunder and falter
> on the way, as long as they live the capacity remains with
> them to create moral standards superior to those their
> fathers evolved. In the annals of our species it has never been
> enough simply to stand still and cling to the past. The moral
> evolution they (the prophets) carried forward acknowl-
> edges no line at which to halt [*The Moral Decision*, p. 314].

Our faith in the moral improvement of human nature might be bolstered by a study of the impact of social and economic changes over the last sixty years on voluntary agencies serving disadvantaged Americans. We are told that "in 1909 the attitude toward the poor was passive, ranging from benign sympathy to complete indifference. Now there is active, sharply quickened social conscience, strong motivation, both individual and official —business, universities, government—toward involvement" (*The New York Times*, May 25, 1969).

That man is destined to rise in the scale of being may be only a hypothesis, but if that hypothesis illumines his past, if it orients him to the present and offers guidance for the future, it should be explored. Religion should help man realize this destiny in terms of spiritual as well as biological survival. *Just as his sex drive extends life for ends beyond those of his own time, so his drive toward self-metamorphosis points to his spiritual living for ends beyond his mortality.* "In satisfying the religious crav-ing," says William E. Hocking, "an individual serves the race more than he serves himself" (*Meaning of God in Human Ex-perience*, p. 49).

Particularly now that the idea of evolution has become in-tegrally associated with all manner of life, the meaning of God in history is enhanced. It denotes that nature's God directs the affairs of men to effect the metamorphosis of the human species. When man's humanity dominates his animal nature, his licentiousness and aggressions will give way to responsibility, war will give way to peace. *The Jewish conception of God as manifest in history and in prophetic intuition implies a metamorphosis in the nature of men and nations which alone can bring about God's Kingdom on earth.*

Summarizing the biblical version, the purpose of Jewish existence is to promulgate the idea that the metamorphosis of man into a human animal can come about only as the end result of ethical nationhood and world peace. Only by accepting ethical nationhood as its wisdom or religion can the Jewish people renew itself.

The following excerpt from a Hanukkah sermon by Alan W. Miller, Rabbi, of the Society for the Advancement of Judaism, throws light on the Jewish sense of destiny:

> *The destiny of the Jewish people is not to be a military people.* Judaism is the evolving *religious* civilization of the Jewish people. The Zionists wanted to normalize the Jewish people. But they failed to comprehend what is normal for the Jewish people. What is normal for the Jewish people is as yet abnormal for other peoples. By normalizing ourselves, by imitating Gentile exemplars, we destroy our very Jewishness and, instead of becoming normal, we become non-existent. We are a diaspora people and a minority people, especially in the Middle East. Not *any* kind of Zionism but only spiritual Zionism, not nationalism but only ethical nationhood, will suffice. *History has cast us into the role of being witnesses of the Divine.* When there is a breakdown in morality in society, the Jews suffer first. They are the thermometer which first registers the fever of society's sickness. When the forces of reaction take over, and the storm clouds of bigotry hover on the horizon, the Jews are the barometer of impending cataclysm. By observing how a nation treats its Jews, we may diagnose that nation's ethical health and condition. By observing how a world of nations, a United Nations, treats a little state like Israel, we may diagnose the sickness of that international body and the sickness of mankind. History, not our own voluntary choice, has made us God's witnesses.
>
> *We cannot normalize the Jewish people. History has made*

of us a people, a collected psycho-social mutant, dependent not upon the ethics of power but upon the power of ethics. This makes us very vulnerable. No one can guarantee that little Jewish children will not again be tormented and burned simply for being Jewish. We have absolutely no alternative, short of collective suicide, a global Jewish Masada, to facing up to what it really means to be a Jew. . . . A reconstituted international Jewish people could show the world what can be achieved by a people without an army, a prototype of what all peoples must become, if humanity is to survive.

The Syrian Greeks are no more. We live to tell the Divine tale. The Romans are no more. We survived to declare the works of the Divine. With our backs to the Cosmic wall, we say to mankind: Learn what we Jews have learned from world history or else, in this nuclear age, we will all perish. If you want to survive meaningfully, albeit through the anguish of vulnerable and potential martyrdom, then repeat after us, the Jewish people, slowly: Not by the ethics of power, but by the power of ethics. Not by might, nor by strength, but by My Spirit, saith the Lord!

Self-metamorphosis as the goal of human striving must not remain a pipe dream. If a universal order of society which outlaws war as it has eliminated dueling is to emerge out of the jungle of our exploitative world, it must be based upon a complete transformation of man's aggressive nature. Religious institutions should take the initiative in launching an all-out educational effort to control man's licentious and combative tendencies before a new and nuclear Armageddon destroys the world. Such education is not a matter of moral slogans and ethical abstractions to be carried out in a vacuum. It must be translated into active endeavor in all areas of human life.

CHAPTER VI

Zionism's Unfinished Business

I. THE NEED FOR AN IDEOLOGY

ZIONISTS should reexamine their ideology. The pattern of ideas which defined Zionist goals in the past no longer suffices in the present situation of world Jewry. Viewing the Jewish world from a broad perspective Zionism should bring order into the variety of Jewish philosophies and programs and point the way to a creative future.

At various stages in its career ancient Israel achieved a spiritual transformation. When the Jewish people in formal assembly accepted certain principles and duties, their conscious and deliberate commitment revitalized Jewish civilization. Might not the adoption now of a comprehensive and illuminating Zionist ideology so revolutionize Jewish life as to effect a genuine renaissance?

In the days of Ezra and Nehemiah the Jewish people transformed themselves into a new kind of human society. By adopting the covenant and laws of the Mosaic Torah they became a *Knessiah*, or theocratic people, which served later as a model for Christendom and Islam. Prior to that act the covenant—which Moses had enacted at Sinai, Joshua reenacted at Shekem and King Josiah at Jerusalem—had marked turning points in the career of ancient Israel. Each new way of life, accepted solemnly as a public act of choice, served as a bond of Jewish unity that has withstood the disintegrative forces of time. Except for the Karaite schism during the Dark Ages, the Jewish people preserved its unity and status. In the ancient sense of an ethnic or kinship group the Jews constituted a nation. Neither exile nor dispersion altered that status.

During the last two centuries the Torah tradition has become inoperative as a uniting factor among the majority of Jews. Their group status has become an enigma. Without a common basis of unity Jews lack a consistent ideology to direct such cooperative efforts as the building of the State of Israel, the organization of communal life in the diaspora or the cultivation of a distinctive life-style. Whatever has been achieved thus far has been the result of impulsive reaction to danger. Without a definite ideology or way of life, how long can Jews exercise the will to live as a united people and to transmit a common cultural and spiritual heritage to posterity? How can they establish a Jewish identity?

Zionism owes its existence to one of many crises which brought the Jewish people to the edge of an abyss. At each critical juncture a new idea emerged which served as a life-saving bridge. There have been four such salvational ideas that saved the Jewish people from extinction on the following critical occasions:

The migration of Jacob and his family to Egypt might have put an end to the existence of the patriarchal group and to its association with the Deity, *Shaddai*. But when Moses came to the Israelites with the mission from the God of their Fathers to redeem them from Egypt, patriarchal history was saved from oblivion and the destiny of the Israelites was confirmed.

The destruction of the First Commonwealth and the Babylonian exile might have put an end to the Jewish people. But the prophets who had anticipated the catastrophe prepared the people both for exile and for ultimate return to their land. If Jewish history survived the Roman annihilation of the Second Commonwealth, it was because Rabban Yohanan ben Zakkai conceived the idea of a portable authority by substituting Torah

for the state. That form of self-government known as nomocracy
—government in accordance with a system of law—preserved the
Jewish people for nearly two millennia.

The convergence in modern Europe of *nationalism* and *naturalism* liberated the forces of anti-Semitism and materialist secularism. Singly or combined these movements in modern dress have
sought to destroy the body and soul of the Jewish people. Zionism—the salvational idea which came to the rescue—released
unsuspected creative powers that had been latent. May the
Jewish people look to Zionism to give them a new lease on life?

What Zionism has achieved so far is monumental; but its
mission has not been accomplished. Apart from the hazards still
faced by the State of Israel, the Jewish people as a whole confronts new dangers to creative survival. Still relevant is the
warning sounded by the British Zionists shortly after the establishment of Israel:

> The State of Israel has solved the problem of the real
> danger that the existence of the State might divide Jewry
> into two separate camps, the Jews of Israel and the Jews
> of the *Golah*, with each camp speaking a different language
> and entertaining different ideas from the other. Should such
> a situation develop, it will be possible to say that while
> Zionism succeeded in creating the State, it lost the People
> of Israel.

In his keynote address at the First American Zionist Assembly
in New York in 1953, Nahum Goldman cautioned:

> It may sound paradoxical, but it may nevertheless be true,
> that Zionism will hereafter be judged by its efforts for
> Jewish survival outside Israel more than by its efforts on
> behalf of Israel . . . No less than our obligations to see
> Israel through its difficult period is our obligation to defeat
> indifference, arrest assimilation, combat disintegration, for
> those dangers are more imminent today than in any previous
> period in our history.

In 1964 at the Twenty-sixth World Zionist Congress in Jerusalem, Goldman declared: "the State of Israel is the main factor
for Jewish life everywhere and the main guarantor for the
survival of the Jewish communities in the world."

The second stage in the fulfillment of Zionism must be as revolutionary as was its first stage. *It must reconstitute and unify the Jewish people and redefine its status vis-à-vis the rest of the world.*

Although Zionists differ on the controversial question of universal *aliyah*, Israel speaks with overwhelming unanimity. Since the World Zionist Congress (Jerusalem, 1964), when the call for mass immigration from Western countries became a mandate, the voice of organized Zionism has been reduced to an echo of the Israeli propaganda line. Such subservience is neither constructive nor honest. It ignores the realities of Jewish life in the diaspora and the need for its creative and dignified survival.

What are the facts? As hitherto formulated, Zionism maintains the traditional belief which negates normal Jewish existence outside Israel. To read a contrary idea into Ahad Ha-Am's cultural or spiritual Zionism is erroneous. In his view the reclamation of *Eretz Yisrael*, beyond creating a haven of refuge, would serve as the instrument of a thoroughgoing Jewish renaissance. He counted on *Eretz Yisrael* to inspire and activate the reeducation of diaspora Jews, awaken their dormant national spirit and impel them to migrate to *Eretz Yisrael*.

Zionists who promulgate the doctrine of *shelilat ha-galut*— the hopelessness of salvaging Jewish life in the diaspora—utter dire warnings of anti-Semitism, even in the United States (which at present harbors almost half of world Jewry). American Jews cannot be persuaded to migrate to Israel *en masse;* the attempt do so is self-defeating and unworthy. By their fallacious assumptions with regard to the futility of Jewish life in the diaspora, Israelis and other Jews aggravate the spiritual crisis. The *will-to-live* is a determining factor for survival. It should be reinforced by every legitimate means, not discouraged.

The Jews of Israel must understand that their future is bound up with the future of world Jewry. For a long time to come, Israel must count for its security and growth on the resources and influence of diaspora Jewry. Diaspora Jewry must see evidence of a reciprocal feeling of fraternity and spiritual kinship from the Jews of Israel. There must be a common understanding with regard to the character and destiny of the Jewish people as well as the future social structure of world Jewry.

Although the disintegrative influences upon Jewish life in the diaspora must be reckoned with, they can be mastered. In the past Jewish society possessed a unique and intense self-awareness. Each individual was permeated with a sense of Jewish unity and responsibility. His beliefs, values and hopes were molded out of the substance of that experience. It is the task of Zionism to revive that experience so that Jews might again become a people in the sense described by J. Pedersen:

> A people is not a collection of human beings more or less like each other. It is a psychical whole, and insofar, an ideal quantity. "The people" is not visible. All common experiences are merged into the common soul and lend to it shape and fullness. Thus a psychic stock is created which is taken over from generation to generation, being constantly renewed and influenced by new experiences. It is lived wholly in every generation and yet it is raised above it, it is something which is given to it and makes claims to it. The connection between the generations of a people is just as intimate as that between the generations of a family. The soul of a people and the soul of the family belong equally to the individual; only their subject differs [*Israel*, p. 475].

The prayer recited every fourth Sabbath ushering in the new month concludes: "All Israel form one fellowship." Such a fellowship "includes both intellectual understanding and the sharing of one another's feelings, the ability to correct and criticize one another understandingly and constructively. It includes the ability and will to cooperate in such manner as to conserve the good of life achieved to date and to provide conditions for its increase" (Henry Wieman, *The Source of Human Good*, p. 64).

The Zionist movement should strive not only for the security and growth of the State of Israel, but also for the unity of the Jewish people throughout the world, for the redefinition of its group status and for the revitalization of the Jewish spiritual heritage. These larger purposes require a formal declaration on the part of the State of Israel which would on the one hand disavow all claims of political loyalty and on the other hand affirm such claims to spiritual loyalty as would be rooted in the common spiritual heritage known as Judaism.

Zionism should inspire many Jews to migrate to Israel and help in its upbuilding. But it should at the same time motivate those who remain behind to perpetuate their Jewish group individuality and foster their spiritual heritage. They should be encouraged to resist those forces in their own environment which tend to alienate them from the Jewish people, from its past achievements and its historic sense of destiny. If their adherence to Judaism and Zionism is to be retained, they must be made to recognize that they need the Jewish people and that the Jewish people needs them.

Why do diaspora Jews need the Jewish people? Because in the diaspora secular society and nation states cannot provide them with those affiliations of family and religious community which are essential to their moral and spiritual orientation. Only through his especial relationship to Jewish family and community can the diaspora Jew be motivated to foster the Jewish spiritual heritage which is to render him kin with the international Jewish people.

But the Jewish people must offer the individual Jew more than an ancient tradition or creedal religion. It cannot afford to echo O'Neill's despair of life: "There isn't any present or future, there is only the past over and over again now" *(A Moon for the Misbegotten)*. It must make traditional religion a civilizing and humanizing force in interpersonal and international relations. *The tradition must be made relevant to the contemporary cultural, economic and sociological needs of human life.* Out of these needs there can well arise both a harmonic and a contrapuntal system of ideas concerning God, man and the world which would revitalize the tradition. That tradition, enhanced in content and vision, would mark the renaissance of the Jewish people and render it morally and spiritually indispensable.

It is obvious that the Jewish people cannot survive without the adherence of the individual Jew. But the Jewish people should not demand exclusive possession of his personality nor insist that he reside in *Eretz Yisrael*. It should recognize the value of Jewish life in two civilizations and the fact that the spiritual allegiance which Jews owe to Jewish civilization is entirely compatible with the political allegiance due the country of which he is a citizen. "The attachment of Jews throughout the world to Israel," said Premier Ben-Gurion in 1957 (several years before he denounced Zionists who did not immigrate), "is based on a joint spiritual and cultural heritage and on a historical sentiment toward the land which was the birthplace of the Jewish people and of its Book." It now devolves upon Zionism to foster that attachment as a spiritual bond which can exercise a dynamic and beneficent influence on Jews everywhere.

A people whose adherents are aware of their mutual need for spiritual well-being, self-perpetuation and destiny is, in the truest and deepest sense of the term, "a people." With freedom of thought and expression a religious people must manage to attain unity within diversity and continuity within change. That achievement should not be difficult because the Jewish people possesses an inexhaustible tradition which, however diversely interpreted, can function as a unifying influence.

In an article in the Jubilee issue of *Hapoel Hatzair*, Israel Cohen described the experiences of the first Zionist settlers in Deganiah:

> They could have failed completely had they not possessed the fundamental traits of pioneers, that of rejecting conventional ideas which had behind them the authority of the most illustrious leaders of their own people, and that of emancipating themselves from socialist principles which also had behind them the authority of great masters of economic theory.

Likewise the Jews of today must create new group concepts to deal with unprecedented conditions. Jewish life under conditions of dispersion in the past, even during the so-called Golden Periods, cannot serve as precedent for the future. In the past segregation enabled Jews to retain their solidarity despite dispersion in different lands. Because they subscribed to one and the same law code, they constituted a nomocracy. *The type of community which Jews must henceforth constitute will have to be a novum, structurally and ideologically.* Structurally, it would resemble a wheel with hub and spokes. The hub would be the Jewish community in Israel, to be known as Zion, while the Jewish communities in the diaspora would constitute the spokes. The rim holding together the entire structure would consist of various strands of belief and practice, all of which would have their source in the Jewish tradition.

Zionist leadership should call a Jewish World Conference to reconstitute the Jewish people. That reconstitution should mark the fourth renewal of the covenant originally entered into on Mount Sinai under the leadership of Moses. It should unite the Jewish people with the new mankind and the nations committed to justice, freedom and universal peace.

This unfinished business is entirely within the scope of the Zionist movement. If the controversy between Herzl's political and Ahad Ha-Am's spiritual Zionism had initially been resolved, an entirely different political as well as spiritual constellation might have come into being with the establishment of the State of Israel. At the very least it would have been unnecessary for the Israeli High Court to hear arguments on the question, Who is a Jew? without being able to arrive at a decision, as was the case in Jerusalem on October 17, 1968. At its best there would have been no need some years ago for the Israeli ministry of education to decree that time be given to the fostering of Jewish consciousness in the sense of unity and common destiny with all Jews throughout the world. As a modern democratic state, unentangled with religious issues, Israel might have permanently forestalled the possibility of a *kulturkampf* which at present only the struggle for mere survival can stave off. There might also have emerged a type of religious patriotism which might not only have unified Jews in the State of Israel but also have become a paradigm of ethical patriotism for the nations of the world.

Under the title "Living History" Nahum N. Glatzer quotes Franz Rosenzweig:

> The fact that we do not live within the laws of world history, or, to state it positively, the fact of our everlastingness, renders all the phases of our history simultaneous. In the history of other peoples, reaching back for what has

been left behind is necessary only from time to time; for us, it is a constant, vital necessity. And we must not forget that it is a *vital* necessity, for we must be able to live within our everlastingness [Franz Rosenzweig: *His Life and Thought*, p. 292].

The status of traditional religion in the polity of the modern nations is relevant to the situation of diaspora Jewry. Some, like Russia and its satellites, repudiate all religions not only because they are traditional, but because they are international. Judaism and Jewish activities are rigorously banned because they assert the corporate identity of Jews within and without the Soviet Union. The survival and the enhancement of Jewish life in the diaspora is dependent upon the understanding and good will of those nations which have worked out a *modus vivendi* between the traditional religions and their own life-styles. Countries like England and the Scandinavian nations which recognize an established religious tradition permit all others. The United States whose constitution prohibits an "establishment of religion" treats all traditional religions with respect.

Only those nations which have granted religious freedom to the various Christian creeds have granted full civic rights to the Jews and given unqualified recognition of the State of Israel. That fact must be borne in mind when Jews wish to achieve universal recognition for their status as a transnational people. If, for example, Zionism were to restrict the Jewish people within the confines of a secular nation in Israel, or if it were to revive the theocracy with the restoration of the Temple, priesthood and sacramental cult, or if it were to negate the possibility of fruitful Jewish life in the diaspora—if Zionism were to adopt any of those three ideologies, it would undermine the good will of the Western nations.

In contrast with Communist nations the political structure and ideologies of the Western democracies are compatible with the will of Jews to constitute a transnational people with its core in the State of Israel. Hence Jewish peoplehood should be identified as a religious category and the Jewish people should be known as a religious community. Only as such a community can it fall into the familiar pattern that smoothes the way for friendly intercourse with those nations without whose friendship Jews would find themselves completely isolated.

Let Zionism attend to its unfinished business—that of reconstituting the Jewish people.

What ground is there for complaint against the State of Israel? In its Declaration of Independence and as a member of the UN Commission on Human Rights, Israel is pledged to the exercise of unqualified religious freedom. But Jews who adhere to the Reform or Conservative version of Judaism are denied recognition, and any public facility or hotel which grants such Jews a place to worship is deprived of its *kashrut* license. The official explanation of such discrimination is that Conservative and Reform Judaism are not authentic. Only those Orthodox rabbis authorized by the government are "qualified" to distinguish between authentic and inauthentic Jews. It is probably only because of the fear of creating a scandal that Reform and Conservative Jews who wish to settle in Israel, are recognized as Jews and citizens.

By their failure to expose and combat this untenable situation the non-Orthodox Jews whose rabbis, when they arrive in Israel, are stripped of their ordination, are guilty of moral evasion. The temporizing and pusillanimous surrender of the Israeli government to the Orthodox group strikes at the heart of Jewish survival. Jews have been denied religious freedom throughout the centuries by the Gentile world and have managed to survive. But it is doubtful whether Judaism can survive in the State of Israel if the Orthodox Jews, who are a minority, continue to dictate the conditions under which other Jews wish to live, thus declaring the overwhelming majority as outside the pale.

Another danger to Jewish survival inheres in the attitude of Zionist negativists who write off all Jews who wish to perpetuate Jewish life outside Israel. Those negativists (and former Prime Minister Ben-Gurion heads the list) deny the rights of Jews to call themselves Zionists, unless they migrate to Israel.

The attitude of the Orthodox in Israel toward non-Orthodox Jews, and that of the Zionist negativists toward Jewish life in the diaspora, jeopardize the survival of the Jewish people.

Could anything be more paradoxical? How is it that Jews have been maneuvered into so anomalous and scandalous a situation?

Before the shock waves of the Eichmann trial, a spiritual gap divided the Jews of the diaspora from those of the State of Israel. To counteract the alienation of the Israeli youth from the rest of world Jewry, the Ministry of Education ordered elementary and secondary school teachers to imbue their pupils with Jewish consciousness. Some of those young people who were products of Jewish education in Israel, made it a point to declare themselves Israelis instead of Jews. By this time, however, a radical change had taken place in Israel-diaspora relations. The spiritual gap between them seems almost to have been bridged by the crisis of the Six-Day War which shocked them into a realization of their mutual dependence for survival.

2. THE RECONSTITUTION OF THE JEWISH PEOPLE

In *Der Judenstaat* published in 1895 Theodor Herzl declared, "We are a people—one people," and the World Zionist movement, which he founded two years later, acted upon that credo. For fifty years Zionists came to the Land of Israel to rebuild and to be rebuilt. But the culmination of their efforts in the establishment of the State of Israel in May 1948 has not clarified the fundamental issues of Jewish peoplehood.

What indeed are the responsibilities of Jews throughout the world to this sovereign state? Have Jews adopted a "second nationality"? What has happened to the traditional concept of *galut* (exile)? Is the State of Israel to be identified with the old yearning for the messianic age? What is the nature of the relationship of one diaspora community to another? Does a sense of interdependence obtain among them, or are they to be regarded as individually bound to Israel but not necessarily in the same spirit to one another?

These unanswered questions continue to plague Jews. Lacking a clearly defined status, intelligent Jews suffer a sense of alienation and self-rejection. The Jewish people is sick unto death. It is in danger of dissolution and absorption by the nations of the world. Only a tremendous effort on the part of spiritually mature Jews can save Jewish civilization. Thus reconstituted, the Jewish people may contribute the same drive to the life of the human spirit in the modern world as it gave to ancient civilizations.

Who is a Jew? The question came before a British court of law when a woman contested the will of her father whose legacy was to be withdrawn if she married a man who was not a member of "the Jewish religion." She married a non-Jew and sued for her father's legacy on the ground that, according to English law—when a condition limiting the grant in a will is vague—it may not be enforced. On appeal the House of Lords ruled (1943) that since it was impossible from the standpoint of religion, race or any other criterion to determine who was a Jew the condition of the will could not be enforced. The daughter won her case.

As a contributor to the anthology *The Jews, Their History, Culture and Religion*, Herskowitz, a well-known Jewish anthropologist, wrote: "Who are the Jews?" His conclusion—"No word means more things to more people than does the word 'Jew' "—was confirmed by an outstanding Conservative Rabbi who asserted that a Jew was "a person who always asks himself, 'What am I?' "

Nor is this quandary confined to the Jews and Gentiles outside the State of Israel. There the Ministry of Education had to direct its instructors to teach "Jewish consciousness," because Israeli children had only a vague idea of what a Jew was and of their own relationship to the Jews of the diaspora. Why does this lamentable situation exist? Because of a fatal blunder on the part of Jewish scholars, it has not been realized that one can no more be a Jew without a publicly recognized *de jure* Jewish people than one can be a soldier without a legally constituted army.

The centrifugal force of civic equality (whether granted or hoped for) and of secularist thought has corroded the bonds which had unified Jews throughout the centuries. Although the Zionist movement and the establishment of the State of Israel have mitigated the disintegrative effect of the open society to which Jewry is exposed, Jewish consciousness and a sense of mutual responsibility survive as vague nostalgic sentimentality. But sentimentality is easily dissipated. It offers little resistance to the temptation to shuffle off Jewish problems and burdens and to sink without trace among the general population.

Is the persistence and ubiquitousness of anti-Semitism sufficient to buttress the solidarity of the Jewish people? Such solidarity is the product merely of a common fate, but not of a common faith. When a common fate is prejudicial to his interests, man tries to escape it. Equally ubiquitous with anti-Semitism, therefore, is the phenomenon of Jews who, lacking a common faith, try to escape identification as Jews.

Jewish history records the story of an organic community that first knew itself as a nation (*goy*), people (*am*), household of Israel (*bet Yisrael*) and since the destruction of the Second Commonwealth, as an ecclesia (in the generic sense of a religious community, *Kenesset Yisrael*). Each of these forms of establishment made the individual Jew heir to the collective memories of his people and its cultural and spiritual life. Of these three types of communal solidarity, world Jewry is now in a position to retain and strengthen only its peoplehood. There is no *de jure* provision for the status of Jews outside the State of Israel. Neither is there an *ecclesia* or religious organization that encompasses the various denominations among Jews.

Ethical monotheism was a distinct contribution of ancient Israel to the universal life and thought of mankind. According to tradition, to "enact justice through law" was the behavioral requirement of the descendants of Abraham when God elected him to be their founder. Such were the beginnings of Hebrew civilization which later took the form of Torah. The Torah consists of a declaration of dependence on God and of a constitution which defines the divine laws to be obeyed by the people of Israel. All Jews must now grasp the full import of Torah as the basis of their spiritual civilization, as the instrument for the improvement of human nature and for the betterment of the human condition throughout the world.

If contemporary Jewish civilization is to function as an instrument of Jewish solidarity, Jews must transpose their tradition into the key of religious humanism and reconstitute themselves structurally as a people. The survival of a tradition or spiritual heritage depends upon its reinterpretation in terms of contemporary experience and world outlook. No nation or people can survive creatively without the inspiration of authentic and mature religion. Man is a gregarious animal and throughout the ages has carried on his struggle for existence through involvement in organic and self-disciplined groups. The collective consciousness of each such group constitutes a god. Hence a meaningful version of religion or knowledge of God is at the very heart of Jewish renewal.

The affirmation at the conclusion of Israel's Declaration of Independence—*Mitok bitahon b'tzur Yisrael anu hotemim* (With trust in the Rock of Israel we sign)—implies religious faith. To believe in God means that every human being has the potentiality to fulfill himself by leaving the world the better and happier for his having lived in it. Insofar as man, in cooperation with his fellowmen, creates the spiritual civilization necessary for that fulfillment, he manifests the divine aspect of the cosmos. His creative activity is spiritual, in that it is both religious and ethical.

A second element of Jewish peoplehood is that its Torah is a three-dimensional culture. It is a way of life or civilizational process; it is a series of writings, which are the product of that process; and it is the cultural instrument for transmitting that product from generation to generation. In psycho-social terms those writings record the efforts of the Jewish people to foster a kind of ethico-religious civilization. Hence the only correct and meaningful definition of Torah is the functional one, namely, as the ethico-religious or spiritual civilization of the Jewish people.

This version is a far cry from the supernaturally revealed Pentateuch of tradition. As with the idea of God, modern Jews are confronted with the problem of maintaining the identity and continuity of a people's civilization despite radical changes in world outlook. To maintain that identity and continuity, a bridge must be built between the ancient and the modern cultural climate. The purpose of achieving salvation or the good and fulfilled life, individually and collectively, might well serve as such a bridge. Jewish peoplehood should foster a moral and spiritual way of life or a Torah form of civilization.

A third implication of Jewish peoplehood is the creative interchange on the part of its adherents who speak the same language and have common interests. Such interchange among individuals posits a land which they possess and over which they exercise autonomy. Peoplehood requires a homeland. That assumption figures prominently throughout Jewish tradition in the role assigned to *Eretz Yisrael*. Whatever might have been the actual circumstances of the conquest of Canaan by the ancient Israelites, there can be no question about its significance. *The land which is a people's home should foster a humanizing way of life. The people that fails to pursue a civilized and enlightened way of life must ultimately be exiled from its homeland.* The narrative parts of Pentateuch and ancient prophecy articulate these ideas concerning the role of *Eretz Yisrael* in the life of the Jewish people. They constitute the basic theme of ancient Israel's epic.

Throughout the past *Eretz Yisrael* functioned as the homeland of the Jews, no matter *where else they happened to live.* Segregated within the nation that harbored them, they continued to observe the way of life which had been fashioned by the landscape and social conditions of *Eretz Yisrael* before the exile of their ancestors. Consequently they experienced a far keener sense of solidarity than any state government could confer upon its citizens.

But Jewish peoplehood today must bring about spiritual solidarity among all Jews wherever they happen to live. Jewish peoplehood must be experienced by the individual Jew, just as it has been conceived through the ages, as Jewish consciousness. Weakened by the acceptance of emancipation and desegregation, the Jewish people must be publicly reconstituted as a people *de jure.* Only the redefinition of Jewish frontiers in human relations and the creation of new social institutions will project for Jews and non-Jews a *living* image of the Jewish people.

Who are the Jews? In 1958 the Israeli government underwent a crisis. Its ministers could not agree on a mutually acceptable authority to settle that question. Over one hundred and eighty scholars were consulted and in the end the opinion of the Israeli Rabbinate, whose authority is recognized by no more than ten per cent of world Jewry, had to be accepted. The danger of a widening rift between the Jews in Israel and those in the diaspora is compounded by the fragmentation of our people into denominations, four religious and one secular, and each of these trends may owe more to anti-Jewish hostility than to Jewish fellowship.

The lack of status is reflected in the sterility of Jewish educational efforts. An educational system which is merely a form of technical training fails to socialize and humanize its students. The American Jewish child has little opportunity to sense the reality of the Jewish people. Without a formal constitution, representative body or registered adherents, its religious and educational institutions are dead ends instead of thoroughfares to a living functioning society.

Only the demonic force of the Holocaust and recrudescent anti-Semitism aroused the collective will to live and to play a continuing role. Anti-Semitism was initiated by spokesmen of the German nation in the nineteenth century and adopted by the entire German nation after the First World War. Under Hitler it became a war without quarter, aimed at the extermination of the Jewish people. Long before anti-Semitism reached that brutal and murderous stage in Germany, the incitement to it had spilled over into European countries. In Russia it put a quietus on all efforts to grant the Jews civil rights and led to pogroms. In France, which had been the first nation to grant civil rights to the Jews, anti-Semitism overwhelmed liberalism and culminated in the notorious Dreyfus Affair.

Out of the realization that the only defense against extinction lay in auto-emancipation and collective action was born the political Zionism of the Basle Program. It was hoped that a Jewish state would serve as a fortress to shelter the Jews from the ravages of anti-Semitism. As long as the State of Israel depends upon the Jews of the rest of the world for its own security, world Jewry can be depended upon to discharge its responsibility for Israel's welfare.

But can Jews afford to leave it at that? Will the awareness of a common fate guarantee a fruitful and creative sense of unity between the Jews of Israel and the Jews of the diaspora, particularly those of the United States who feel secure (that is, prior to the new dispensation of Black anti-Semitism and its "new left" cheerleaders)? It must be remembered that even the dormant sense of a common fate, which Herzl's Zionism aroused, could not have survived without the functioning memory of a common religion and a self-conscious people for thirty centuries. Now that Herzlian Zionism has fulfilled its goal with the establishment of the State of Israel, Jews must create a Greater Zionism to reconstitute themselves into a living, interactive and creative people.

Utilizing the interest in and concern for Israel, Greater Zionism should call upon the Jews as a transnational people to reformulate their way of life in keeping with the principle of Torah as an evolving religious civilization. The Zionist movement is the logical instrument to promote the reaffirmation of Jewish peoplehood among all other Jewish agencies and organizations. The establishment of the State of Israel is only the first stage in the attainment of that goal. World Jewry as a body should formulate a constitution for the Jews as a transnational people. "A community without law," it has been said, "is but an empty shell." Among the provisions for such a constitution would be the following:

It should define the relation of the Jewish people to existing political bodies, and refute the charge of dual allegiance preferred against Jews living outside the State of Israel.

It should reassert the historic right of the Jewish people to the Land of Israel as its spiritual homeland.

It should affirm that the State of Israel is the creation of the Jewish people for the express purpose of establishing a Jewish community to be known as Zion, which is to function as the spiritual catalyst for Jewish life everywhere.

It should point the way to Judaism an an evolving religious civilization, which is compatible with unity in diversity* and with continuity in change. While allowing for full participation in the life of the nations of which Jews are citizens, it should recognize the inevitable difference in scope and intensity between Jewish life in the State of Israel and in the diaspora.

It should stress the need for a two-way passage between the Jews within the State of Israel and those outside it in all aspects of economic, cultural, scientific and spiritual life.

It should call upon the State of Israel to guarantee for all its citizens freedom of worship as well as freedom of expression in cultural and socio-economic spheres.

It should call for the structuring of Jewish populations in the diaspora on lines of organic community in which every Jew is registered and in which all activities, institutions and organizations are coordinated.

It should call upon each organic Jewish community: (1) to reinstate the ancient Jewish attitude toward the study of Torah as "our life and the length of our days"; (2) to promulgate highly ethical standards on the part of its adherents; (3) to provide for the health, well-being, employment and social welfare of its members by cooperating with local government agencies; and (4) to enlist the talents of those who are able to enhance the ideological and cultural expression of Jewish life.

It should provide for the establishment of three democratically elected and constituted bodies—legislative, judicial and executive —to administer the affairs of the Jewish people as a whole and of each organic Jewish community outside Israel.

It should empower those in charge of both overall and local community affairs to exercise the right of taxation or some other corporate method of financing, within the limits of justice and feasibility, as a means of defraying the cost of administration.

*"Disagreement, controversy and even competitive striving have a positive function in human existence. For how can a man know who he is and what he thinks and believes, unless there are others who think and believe differently?" (*Human Aggression* by Anthony Storr, p. 57).

Mankind should live by voluntarism and personal commitment rather than coercion. Why should not Jews set an example as pioneers of that ethical principle? For more than a century Jews throughout the world have carried on, voluntarily and without legal coercion, gigantic undertakings in philanthropy, education, religion and state-building. Why should not these undertakings be formalized through permanent and effective organizational machinery?

The organic approach to Jewish peoplehood would not supplant existing religious and fraternal organizations or existing federations and community councils. On the contrary, it would reinforce their authority and enhance their moral and spiritual effectiveness. Thus the prophet Ezekiel exhorted his fellow exiles in Babylon: "Get yourselves a new heart and a new spirit! Why should you die, O House of Israel?" (18:31).

The establishment of a Jewish world parliament would create an authority to speak to and for the entire Jewish people and to maintain a high ethical standard in all human relations and activities.

The reorganization of local and regional communities should reflect the spiritual character of world Jewry as a whole. Each such community, rather than an individual congregation, could rightly be designated as *Kehillah Kedoshah* (a holy community), since it would embody the entire spectrum of cultural activities. Only the organic community endows the Jewish people with visible identity.

The present condition of American Jewish communities is not calculated to sustain Jewish life, much less to enhance it. Each generation is less Jewish than the preceding. Leon A. Jick, Director of the Philip W. Lown School of Judaic Studies, wrote:

> An overview of American Jewish history reveals that each "wave of immigration" experienced an initial phase of personal and social disintegration, that each assimilated rapidly, creating institutions which in widely divergent ways, responded to the American situation in its time, that each achieved an institutional and ideological stability which sustained it for a short time, and that thereafter each was propelled into a crisis of identity and continuity. If this generalization is sustained, then we are today in a situation which is

analogous to that of the Sephardic American Jewry in the early 1800's and of German American Jewry in the early decades of this century [*Jewish Frontier,* January 1968].

The self-alienation of the most creatively minded Jews is ominous for the future of American Judaism. A properly devised organic structure of Jewish communal life might counteract those disintegrative forces and harmonize the rasping paradoxes of Jewish life. Among the important communal activities would be the compilation of vital statistics, the maintenance of all-day secondary Jewish schools, provision for arbitration on the manifold problems of social justice.

The practice of adopting Hebraic personal names has a psychological influence as identification with the Jewish people.

So great a dimension of peoplehood is built into observance of the Sabbath and the festivals that they should be revitalized. A Sabbath-less people cannot possibly cultivate the life of the spirit. The revival of the observance of *kashrut,* Sabbaths and festivals would revitalize the action symbols associated with ritual practices and worship. Such observance, together with a workable number of Jewish books, are indispensable to the core of Jewish life—a Jewish home.

Another action symbol is required to deepen the awareness of spiritual unity, namely a higher degree of confirmation—*Ben* and *Bat* Torah—to be conferred at maturity, supplementing the elementary degrees of *Bar* and *Bat* Mitzvah, now conferred at adolescence. We may deplore the fact that congregational attendance at Sabbath services seems to depend on *Bar* and *Bat* Mitzvah occasions, but we must admit they have become indispensable. The degree of *Ben* and *Bat* Torah, conferred upon the acquisition of a working knowledge of Judaism, would more effectively foster Jewish consciousness and spiritual unity.

Unless nations voluntarily limit their individuality and absolute sovereignty the current world situation could lead to the extinction of mankind. By resuming peoplehood as a spiritual dimension Jews may articulate the need for each nation to regard national individuality as a divine gift rather than demonic power.

CHAPTER VII

American Jewry's
Unfinished Business

I. THE COMMUNAL ORGANIZATION OF AMERICAN JEWRY

AMERICAN Jewry is far from being creatively adjusted to the American environment. No minority group can consider itself adjusted, or in a position to live normally and make the best use of its life, unless it is both culturally differentiated from the majority group and economically integrated into it.

To be culturally differentiated does not mean to be segregated from the cultural life of the majority. No such objective is even contemplated for the American Jew. Nothing that is historically, culturally or esthetically valuable in the pattern of American life should be omitted from the texture of the American Jewish consciousness. But assimilating the best in the American environment does not imply the negation of Jewishness. It does not preclude the Jew from fostering his own historical, national and spiritual values to a *maximum* degree compatible with his life as an American. Merely praying as a Jew is not the maximum. The majority of those Jews who affirm that prayer constitutes the maximum Jewish self-expression do little praying. They do many other things which keep them Jewish and which are not provided for in their philosophy. They still refrain, for the most part, from intermarrying; they form clubs to which a Gentile is as ineligible as a financially or socially disqualified Jew; and they bury their dead in Jewish cemeteries. These negative measures do not by themselves constitute creative adjustment. They lack the positive dimension of cooperation for social welfare, encouragement of the arts and the advancement of some ethical or spiritual ideal in the name of Judaism.

While American Jews are almost completely acculturated, the overwhelming majority are ignorant of their spiritual heritage. Their lay leaders are Jewishly illiterate. Not only are they unfamiliar with the classic texts of Judaism and modern Hebrew literature, but they do not follow current English language publications on Jewish subjects. In consequence, the Jews have become traditionless. They have lost all sense of a common past and do not look forward to a common future. They are without any feeling of reverence for Jewish customs, events, persons, writings, festivals and holy days which are hallowed by sacred memories and associations.

To effect the normal adjustment of American Jewry to the cultural life of their country, Jews must accept and implement the ideal of organic Jewish community. *Now that the rest of the world is, for good or for ill, becoming collectivist, Jews must respond with a collectivism of their own, otherwise they are doomed to spiritual disintegration.* This is not merely a matter of organizational machinery or fiscal efficiency; it is basically a psychological problem. Jews must wean themselves away from the tendency to regard "rugged individualism" as a virtue, when as a matter of fact it can easily become a vice. The emancipation of the Jews came as a corollary of the rugged individualism and the *laissez-faire* policy which the expanding economy of the nineteenth century made possible. Then it was important that everyone with ability, irrespective of descent or religion, should be encouraged to apply his initiative and energy to the manifold opportunities in the world of commerce and industry. Jews were permitted to enlarge the scope of their economic activities on what seemed like an equal footing with their neighbors.

Human beings tend to favor policies which proffer some advantage. They soon come to consider such advantage as sacred rights and to resent change, however socially beneficial, as an infringement of those rights and a menace to the moral order. Attributing their good fortune to individualism, successful Jews are conditioned to regard the *status quo* as sacrosanct. With the secular world experimenting with various forms of cooperation, Jews, too, must repudiate extreme forms of individualism which the rest of the world is repudiating as irrelevant to the art of living in society.

The cultivation of spiritual fellowship should check unbridled competition and foster cooperative and creative effort. Such striving for associated life constitutes the most socialized use of the desire to belong. The need for belonging, often ridiculed as herd instinct, is a fundamental and ennobling human trait. It takes the form of a demand for status, self-respect and wholesome adjustment to life.

The sense of status is the awareness of being needed and of being helped in all that one can achieve. Whereas associations for specific purposes such as worship, philanthropy, education or recreation can help a person attain specific objects, only a comprehensive organic community can confer status and dignity upon its adherents. By bringing into play the entire personality of its members the organic community helps each individual attain self-fulfillment or salvation.

The American people as a whole cannot give the Jew that sense of status. The assumption that the Jew can achieve status by patterning his behavior, with the exception of religion, after that of the Gentiles has been disproven. For one thing the majority group whose habits he imitates denies such identification. Nor can it do otherwise. Christian America has been conditioned from early childhood by its religious tradition. Christians cannot respond with reverence to the objects sanctified by Jewish tradition. A *sefer torah* is to them only a scroll of parchment, an interesting museum piece that evokes no more emotion than an Egyptian papyrus. The rites of a Jewish Passover *seder* strike them as quaint and exotic. But they would find no significance in the ritual commemorative of the Jewish past, for it is not *their* past and offers no inspiration to present action. Similarly, the Jew who has been conditioned by his religious tradition cannot respond to the objects and events which Christian tradition has sanctified. The person of Jesus may command his respect but not his adoration; he associates the Cross with persecution rather than salvation. Although the Jew may join in the Christmas rush, which has secularized and commercialized the holiday, he cannot participate with devout Christians in their religious celebration of Christmas.

As long as religion exercises any influence upon Christians, it must give rise to a sense of mutual otherness. While that feeling need not be one of antipathy, it conveys a marked differentiation of identity. In the best sense, difference in identity is compatible with mutual respect and friendliness. But such awareness inhibits Jew and Gentile from looking to the other group for the fellowship that gives status to the individual. Only in his own group can each find the authentic core of his being.

Those Jews who sought assimilation through conversion have, in most cases, been thwarted by an atavistic consciousness of their Jewish origins. "I have been baptized but not converted," wrote Heinrich Heine. Modern anti-Semitism does not even allow the loophole of apostasy as escape from the minority to the majority group. The race theory which makes Jewishness a hereditary taint precludes any voluntary act on the part of the Jew to eradicate or mitigate its effects.

Despite the denigration of prejudice among the cultured élite, most Gentiles resent the Jew who seeks status in Christian society. The fact that the Jew makes notable contributions to the general culture does not make him more acceptable. The recent identification of the Intellectual Establishment as Jewish arouses fear of domination among the less enlightened. It was precisely those Jews who contributed most to the culture of the Weimar Republic who were victimized by Nazi Germany.

Unless Jews are to be spiritually homeless they must seek fellowship in an organized Jewish community life. And so strong must the feeling of fellowship become, so vigorously must it function, that it will transcend all the existing divisions in Jewish life. *There must be a place in the Jewish community for every one who wishes to be a Jew, regardless of his theology or economic condition.* Jews should not compel uniformity of belief and opinion which would impede progress. But those who differ on Jewish policies must not sever relations with others and conduct Jewish affairs as autonomous entities. Freedom of speech must be allowed, but Jews must remain on speaking terms. The will to act in concert for the mutual advantage of all Jews must actuate all parties, however differently they may conceive of these advantages.

The assimilatory policy of those in the upper echelons of wealth or intellect is largely prompted by their desire for social advancement and professional careerism. Some oppose the public discussion of social questions from the pulpit and even from the lecture forums of Jewish community centers for fear of disturbing the *status quo*. The deference paid to religion in public utterances is not reflected in their devotions, which are limited to an occasional visit to the synagogue on High Holy Days and on the anniversary of a death in the family. Similarly their interest in charity may be explained as at least in part motivated by the satisfactions which come from feeling that others are dependent on them. And their opposition to more democratic forms of Jewish social control arises from reluctance to cede the power and prestige which wealth bestows.

A second human need for satisfaction of which Jews as a minority group are dependent upon one another is the need for self-respect. When an individual is deprived of the sense of his own worth his subconscious mind will drive him to re-establish human dignity no matter how illusory the basis. As members of a minority group, Jews may often resort to the mechanisms of irrational defense in the effort to preserve self-respect.

Not content with curtailing the economic opportunities of minorities in their power, majorities attempt to justify their oppression by stigmatizing the weaker group with the label of inferiority. Since every group has its quota of undesirables and instances of individual misbehavior, and since any divergence from conventional behavior patterns can be held up to ridicule, the beliefs and mores of the minority often become associated, even in the minds of its own members, with a sense of shame and contempt. As a reflex, "What would the Gentiles say?" often operates as the first criterion of Jewish policy. The individual Jew must place his own, not Gentile, evaluation upon the Jewish way of life if he is to save his self-respect and spiritual sanity.

That task is more difficult today than it was in the past. When organized religion was dominant and both Church and Mosque cited the Jewish scriptures as well as their own sacred writings in support of their respective confessions, the Jewish people had no difficulty in proving its claim to being God's chosen. By the admission of its rivals, ancient Israel enjoyed sole possession of the key to salvation. Following up on this major premise Judaism asserted that no change had taken place in the divine scheme. The conviction of ultimate vindication imbued Jewish suffering with the dignity of martyrdom. It was not the soul-destroying sense of futility and impotence that characterizes Jewish malaise in modern times. The Jew no longer has faith in the traditional religious sanctions on which the theory of the choice of Israel was predicated. As long as both Jew and Gentile looked for salvation to some transcendent world, the Jew found solace in the belief that he would be compensated for his loyalty to the Torah in the world to come. But with the erosion of this naive belief, Jew, as well as Gentile, has become engrossed in this-worldly pursuits. Finding himself hampered at every step, he expects the Jewish people to resolve his predicament in this-worldly fashion.

The modern Jew, who cannot accept the traditional belief in revelation, must seek true self-knowledge by reassessing his own cultural and spiritual traditions. But the individual cannot accomplish this in isolation. As part of a Jewish community which, by a rich and well-planned communal program of educational and cultural activities, makes the Jewish heritage available, the individual Jew will acquire self-knowledge and spiritual orientation.

Finally, Jewish fellowship is indispensable to the individual as a means of achieving his wholesome adjustment to life. Man envisages his personal life not as confined to the years between birth and death, but as part of a cosmic process. Who can feel that his past began at birth? His physiognomy reflects the features of his parents; his earliest responses to his environment are conditioned by the home which had been prepared in anticipation of his coming; and his wants and thoughts are articulated in a language that generations long dead had created. How can he look upon his life as ending with his death when so many of his acts focus upon the survival of the group? Love, marriage, childbirth and child care manifest vital concern for the future. These traits incline man to an essentially religious being; they link his life to the life of the universe. The stress which religion puts on the immortality of the soul answers the human need to regard life in transcendent terms. Although most thoughtful people may reject the traditional doctrine of personal immortality, they generally experience the need for that quasi-immortality in the stream of personal life which flows from an ancestral source and continues through descendants after death. Immortality for the Jew can be none other than through the Jewish people.

If their respective religious backgrounds inhibit Jews and Gentiles from merging into a single group it is because religion impels the individual to seek adjustment to life as a whole through identification with the group in whose history he is rooted. That is why the commemorative rites of one's own religion are so alive and those of other religions so dead. "One should always look upon himself as if he in person participated in the exodus from Egypt," says the Passover *Haggadah*. That is how the Jews feel on Passover. Somewhere among that multitude of emancipated slaves they uncover the roots of their own being. The Gentile lacks such emotional ties to the observance of Passover.

But while deeply interested in their past, Jews cannot escape concern for the future. They regard themselves as the heirs of the unachieved purposes of the Jewish people, of its unfulfilled ideals. To the extent that he realizes that his personal lifetime is not adequate for their achievement, he looks to posterity to carry out his incompleted social projects. That is how the Jewish instinct of self-preservation functions socially as an instinct for the preservation of the social group. Keenly aware of those who share the heritage of unfulfilled hopes and yearnings which emanate from the past, Jews seek fellowship and cooperation in projecting a common future. The cosmopolitan Jew who is rooted in no people (not even his own), who lacks historic memories, prophetic hopes and objects of reverence, who never experiences communion with fellow Jews who share his ideals, is a sorry creature indeed. Life holds little for him, and death ends all. This cynical and detached observer of the lives of others cannot share in the unending life process that in each generation triumphs over death and decay. He is the consummate product of Jewish individualism. Only a vigorous Jewish community organization can save the Jew from that fate which is the equivalent of *karet*—excision from the organic life of the spirit.

Effective Jewish cooperation demands a change in the psychology of the individual Jew and a corresponding change in Jewish organizations and institutions. Although most Jews feel the need of belonging to some Jewish organization—be it a congregation, fraternal order, philanthropic institution or Zionist society—such institutions do not mitigate the spirit of individualism nor do they promote cooperation and collectivism. As "joiners," Jews are usually motivated by individualistic considerations. A man may join an organization because it enhances his prestige, or furthers his professional or political career, or offers a more effective defense against the hostility of the outside world. But such considerations offer a defensive rather than creative adjustment to the American environment.

The individualistic motivation of the membership fosters a spirit of competition among these organizations. *Jewish institutions and movements jostle one another in an indecent and ruinous scramble for prestige and financial support.* Institutional individualism creates the illusion of belonging; the reality does not exist. Jews imagine that the petty activities of such organizations enhance their status and self-respect. The truth is that not one nor all of these organizations together fulfill the need for Jewish fellowship.

Those who insist that religion is the only common interest of Jews regard affiliation with the synagogue as satisfying the need for Jewish fellowship. Can the synagogue fill that need? Although congregations and their buildings for worship have proliferated in number and ostentation, their hothouse growth has increased disunity. Organized by small homogeneous groups, synagogues reflect their members' religious opinions and preferences as to ritual, as well as their economic and social standards. How can such cliques motivate their members to transcend the ideological and economic barriers that divide the Jewish people? Multiple cleavages give rise to numerous congregations, each of which regards the others as competing rather than as cooperating institutions. And even if by some miracle all congregations were to be combined, their total membership would not begin to include all who consider themselves Jews. Synagogue membership is confined mainly to the upper and middle classes. Is the Jewish worker to be excluded from Jewish fellowship if he cannot subscribe to some synagogue's religious tenets or because he would feel uncomfortable among their affluent worshipers?

The synagogue cannot satisfy the Jewish need for self-respect through identification wth the historic people of Israel. Congregations are too small and too limited in scope to imbue their members with the feeling of participating, however vicariously, in the spiritual and creative achievements of the Jewish people. To the extent that the synagogues are committed to the notion that religion alone makes Jews Jewish, they deprecate the secular interest in the economic welfare of Jews and in the encouragement of esthetic creativity. But these activities are necessary, if the Jew is to feel that he can function as a Jew in every field of human endeavor. He cannot respect a religion that takes no cognizance of them; and such a religion cannot help him reestablish his self-respect which has suffered so much from the assaults of the outside world.

Above all, the synagogue fails when it permits the individualistic competitive spirit to commercialize and degrade religion. When synagogues become rich men's clubs, when the rabbi is expected to be a go-getter and a good mixer, or is valued solely for his oratorical virtuosity, when public functions are exercises in vulgarity and extravagance, the synagogue cannot promote wholesome Jewish adjustment to life.

It cannot even fulfill its specific function—the religious orientation of the Jew. By sanctifying the ideals, events, literary classics, personalities and objects of Jewish history, the traditional synagogue did help to orient the Jew by endowing him with immortality through his self-identification with the Jewish people. But for over a century Jews have been indoctrinated with the idea that they were not a people with an authentic civilization, but a denomination. Jewish unity was based not on their self-identification with a social organism but on their acceptance of a common creed. This notion has reduced religion to a few moral platitudes or to a multitude of legalistic precepts—all predicated on the acceptance of a definite religious philosophy. For those who reject this philosophy—and their number is legion —the ritual of the synagogue has lost its significance. As at present constituted, that ritual can no longer help them get their bearings in life nor proffer the serenity and peace of mind which enables man to transcend his petty cares and vulgar ambitions.

Many have pinned their hopes for the development of a sounder Jewish community life on the Jewish philanthropic federations. These appeal to a larger and more varied constituency than any congregational unit and are effecting some measure of cooperation among social service institutions. But they too are inadequate to create Jewish fellowship. They cannot confer upon the individual Jew spiritual status because they cannot transcend the lines of economic cleavage that divide the Jewish people into a benefactor and a beneficiary class. Such class division strikes at the very roots of Jewish fellowship, which, in the context of mutual helpfulness, is inconsistent with the dependence of one part of the population on another. The irksomeness of this dependence is seen in the dissatisfaction of the beneficiaries with the red tape and officiousness endemic in the operations of organized charity.

Nor can philanthropic federations satisfy the need for Jewish self-respect. Their whole emphasis is on the mitigation of social evils rather than on the achievement of social objectives that express the positive values of Jewish group life. Indeed, they often tend in light of their fiscal interests to resent and prevent the emergence of new Jewish interests, thus inhibiting, rather than encouraging, Jewish creativity along social and cultural lines. As for satisfying the need for wholesome adjustment to life, they do not even make any attempt to do so, relegating this responsibility to the synagogue, with which they have no organic relationship whatsoever. Although the Zionist movement recognizes the principle of organic unity and the need for Jewish fellowship without reference to religious beliefs, it has failed to satisfy Jewish spiritual needs. Immersed in the tasks of nation building, Zionism has not addressed the problem of the satisfactory adjustment of the diaspora Jew to his social environment. The work of interpreting the place of Israel in the scheme of Jewish life has fallen largely to the lot of the synagogue and the Jewish school.

Jewish educational institutions, although serving an indispensable need, cannot by themselves meet all the requirements of Jewish communal life. The program of the Jewish school must seem exotic and irrelevant if its objectives are not defined by Jewish life as lived by the adult Jewish community. The disintegration of the Jewish community has diminished the effectiveness of the Jewish school. The uncertainty of adults as to a Jewish future has eroded interest in Jewish education.

Other useful forms of Jewish organization, such as fraternal orders, youth groups, community centers and service organizations, cannot effect Jewish adjustment to the American environment. While these institutions represent important aspects of Jewish life, they function as if they represented the whole. They do not combine in a corporate entity in which each functions as an organ of the whole and in continuous collaboration with all its other vital organs. The creation of a comprehensive Jewish organism is required to establish the principle of Jewish *collectivism* in place of the present personal and institutional individualism.

Jewish life cannot yield its potential of manifold satisfactions unless it be molded into an organic community. Today there is no Jewish community. Jews imagine that they are continuing the Jewish life of the past, in a modified form to be sure, but continuing it. But the present form of communal organization is as much like the Jewish community of the past as the household furniture in a moving van is like the home before stripped of furnishings. Like the new home which must be set up, the various Jewish institutions should be reassembled in conformity with a general plan and purpose. Only then will they recapture that beauty of form and function which pertains to creative communal life. A Jewish community would make the individual Jew feel that his group is actively concerned in enabling him to attain the maximum of personal self-realization.

This idea of the religiously and ethically motivated community is one of the most significant contributions of the Jewish people to civilization. All the great religious bodies were designed to effect the "salvation" of the individual. But what is salvation if not self-realization through the fulfillment of all those hopes, desires and longings whose frustration lies at the heart of all human misery? The Jewish community must provide its members with the opportunity for utilizing their abilities. It must remove the handicaps—physical, mental and social—that prevent the full exercise of their powers, and so orient the individual to his natural and social environment that he shall feel secure and at home in the world.

The Functions of a Jewish Community Organization

A Jewish community organization capable of satisfying the need for Jewish status, self-respect and wholesome adjustment to life must envisage the problem of Jewish life in its entirety. No Jewish interest can be alien to it. Its functions may be considered under six heads: administrative, economic, cultural, social service, public relations and political.

1. *Administrative functions:* Every adult Jew who wishes to identify as such should register in the community and pay nominal annual dues. These dues must be so low as to make it possible for every Jew, regardless of his economic status, to become a member of the community. It goes without saying that no discrimination must be made on the basis of religious belief. Similarly, no discrimination should be made on the basis of one's political or social opinions. Personal registration as a member of the Jewish community should be a prerequisite to taking part in its activities or enjoying the privileges of membership, such as participating in communal elections, being married with a Jewish ritual or receiving Jewish burial.

The Jewish community organization should control the raising of funds for Jewish communal purposes and their proper administration to avoid waste and duplication and to insure a proper apportionment of the budget for all Jewish needs.

The community organization should make provision for the employment of the highest type of personnel available in the professional, executive, clerical and other forms of service required by the community. It should provide for the training of rabbis, cantors, educators, social workers, institutional executives, *shohetim, mohelim* and the like. Where it is more expedient to depend on national institutions for such training, it should include in its budget an adequate contribution to such institutions. All these functionaries and employees should be employed and paid by the community, which should define their duties, the terms of their employment and the standards of service.

The Jewish community should establish an agency for the registration of Jewish vital statistics: marriages, divorces, births, deaths and other important personal data. This is necessary not alone for the compiling of vital statistics which are essential to social work, but also to give the Jew that sense of status which comes from his awareness that the Jewish community regards his personal life as an organic part of the life of the group. The Jewish community should provide the social research to establish a factual basis for dealing with the complex problems of Jewish life. Without accurate data and expert evaluation, the determination of Jewish policy is apt to be based on wishful thinking, personal prejudice and partisan passion.

2. *Economic functions:* The Jewish community organization should aim to remove, or at least mitigate, the handicaps and discrimination which Jews experience in their economic life.

3. *Cultural functions:* The Jewish community organization should provide Jewish educational facilities for child, adolescent and adult to encourage literary and artistic creativity and to provide for public worship and other forms of religious activity. Prerequisite to such an educational program is the establishment of a bureau of Jewish education. Although the diversity of religious and social viewpoint among Jews precludes the establish-

ment of a uniform and homogeneous system of education, Jewish education should not be condemned to further disintegration and ineffectuality. Bureaus of education can raise standards by providing for the training, licensing and appropriate scale of remuneration for Jewish teachers. They should supervise and advise Jewish schools of every type, showing them how they can adjust their programs to the needs of the Jewish community as a whole. They can improve the quality of school buildings and equipment by developing standards of hygiene, sanitation and esthetics. They can provide textbooks and other educational materials and stimulate creative and inspiring inter-school activities. They should acquaint the adult members of the Jewish community with the vital need for Jewish education if their children are to fulfill all their potentialities for happy and useful living.

The Jewish community should encourage the organization of clubs for young people to deepen their commitment to the Jewish cultural heritage. Adolescents and young people should participate in the social and cultural activities for the service of the community.

Community centers should utilize Jewish cultural material to stimulate the creative activity of Jews of all ages in every avenue of cultural and social endeavor. They should foster the arts and sciences and all forms of social action for the welfare of the Jewish group, the general community and all humanity. The Jewish community center must function as a force for integrating Jewish tradition with the cultural needs of the general community, thus making a distinctive contribution to American life.

The Jewish community should undertake a varied program of cultural activities, such as lecture forums, study circles, libraries, art exhibitions and exhibits. It should encourage Jewish literature, the Jewish press, Jewish music and drama. It should seek collaboration with the public school system and with colleges for the teaching of Jewish subjects such as Hebrew and Jewish history. The curricula of colleges which offer religious instruction should include scholarly courses in Jewish religion.

The Jewish community should alert the communications

media to the cultural significance of the public celebration of Jewish holidays.

4. *Social service functions:* These functions of the Jewish community should embrace most of those activities which are now the main concern of our local philanthropic federations. The Jewish community will have to provide hospitalization and nursing service for the sick and make institutional provision for the blind, deaf, crippled and all who are physically or mentally handicapped. Even where the State takes over the major responsibility for such provision, the Jewish community will remain under the obligation to provide for the Jewish needs of those who are so handicapped. The care of all dependent classes of the Jewish population, such as orphans, the aged, refugees from persecution, and so on, will likewise be a responsibility of the Jewish community. Nor must the social service activities of the Jewish community be confined to the satisfaction of local needs. Movements for overseas relief and the facilitation of Jewish migration wherever necessitated by economic or political pressure must be locally sponsored by the Jewish community organization.

5. *Public relations functions:* Since a spiritual center of Jewish life is basic to the entire concept of Jewish peoplehood, the Jewish community organization must organize support for Israel. Diaspora Jews live in two civilizations, their own and that of the majority population whose centrifugal pull threatens Jewish survival as a distinct entity. But the establishment of an autonomous nation with a complete and unhyphenated Jewish culture generates centripetal forces to restore the normal balance of the Jewish people, giving it dignity and status.

6. *Political functions:* Although self-constituted Jewish bodies have done valiant service in the defense of Jewish rights, none has authority to speak in behalf of organized Jewry. If Jews were organized in local communities whose representatives sat in a democratically elected national body, Jewish demands would acquire the force of a mass movement and Jewish leaders could bring tremendous pressure to bear in their assertion of Jewish rights.

Moreover, a responsible Jewish community organization could discourage individual careerists from injecting false Jewish issues into American political life. The present state of disorganization affords opportunity to unscrupulous adventurers to exploit Jewish institutions for selfish ends. Only an efficient and democratically organized Jewish community can control this situation, and the exercise of such control would contribute immeasurably to Jewish welfare.

The foregoing statement of the functions of the Jewish community is by no means exhaustive, but it gives some indication of the benefits which we may expect from a well-ordered Jewish communal life. Opponents of the kind of social structure which would mediate the reality of the Jewish people for the individual Jew are obsessed with the fear of a return to the ghetto.

Most of the objections on ideological grounds assume that the Jew is to be assimilated to the rest of the American population in respect to everything but religion. If those who hold this view took religion seriously, they would not find in the promotion of the secular interests of Judaism sufficient ground for opposing Jewish communal life. Every sincere religionist seeks not to segregate religion from all other human interests, but to make religion dominate them. All religious fellowships feel the responsibility of securing the fullest measure of salvation to all who are born into their community.

Those who exclude Jewish religion from the process of complete cultural absorption are not eager to see Jewish religion dominate Jewish life. What they really desire is the liquidation of everything that is distinctively Jewish. If they exempt Judaism from liquidation, it is because religion and its institutions are revered in America. Since it is psychologically difficult for Jews to subscribe to other faiths without a shamefaced feeling of disloyalty, they affiliate with Jewish religious institutions, for fear of forfeiting the respect of the Gentiles. *Jews who are not religious and pay only a formal deference to religion* are blocking the channels of vital contact with the day-by-day interests and activities of the Jewish people. If the synagogue is the heart of the Jewish organism, one should not sever the arteries through which it sends the bloodstream to every member of the body.

Others object that an integrated Jewish community would expose American Jews to the charge of hyphenism. That such a charge may be brought cannot be denied. But this should not act as a deterrent. The only alternative for the Jew who seeks adjustment to the American environment is complete assimilation. Even if the establishment of Jewish community organizations were resented by non-Jews—a fantastic supposition—it would still be the duty of Jews to organize their community life in accordance with their highest ideals. Characteristic of the Jewish inferiority complex are the Jews who "flee when no man pursueth." The American theory of government opposes the totalitarian state. The assumption by the government of a measure of responsibility for the welfare of its citizens has never been interpreted as giving the state the right to monopolize such activity. The legitimacy of groups organized on a voluntary basis, not merely for the promotion of public worship but for the promotion of common cultural and social interests, has never been questioned.

Equally fantastic is the notion that Jewish communal organization would lead the Jew back into the ghetto. It is an ineluctable fact that the Jews in America share in the economic, political, cultural and social life of the country. American Jews are neither able nor willing to segregate themselves from the non-Jewish population. They want to vote at the same polls, speak the same language, attend the same schools and colleges and go to the same theaters and other places of amusement as the Gentiles. And they accept their share of moral responsibility for all organized efforts at advancing the common interests of the people of their city, state and nation.

But all Jews who are affirmatively Jewish—and no others should have the right to direct Jewish social policy—want to maintain some continuity with the Jewish past. They have a common faith in the potentialities of Jewish life for the future; they wish to keep in contact with their fellow Jews throughout the world; they desire to raise their children as Jews; and they seek to effectuate the spiritual ideals inherent in their Jewish heritage and group life. An organization that will implement these common interests of American Jews, over and above whatever interests they share with the rest of the American population, involves no segregation. It imposes no narrowing adherence to specific dogma. It puts no fetters on freedom of thought and artistic self-expression. It is predicated on no assumption of racial superiority. It seeks no exclusive economic or political advantages. Wherein then does it mean a return to the ghetto?

Indeed, Jewish community organization provides the only way out of the ghetto. The failure of the non-Jewish world to permit the Jews to share a more intimate social communion has imposed a sense of inferiority on most Jews. Rebuffed by the Gentiles, they compensate for the hurt to their self-respect by exaggerated pretensions to superiority. Some withdraw to the friendly protection of a purely Jewish milieu and avoid the enriching contact with other cultures. Others, in resentment against Gentile exclusion, grow to hate the Jews and all things Jewish. They find refuge in a ghetto within a ghetto, inhabited by other Jews who have fled from Judaism. Only by making Jewish community life meaningful can the Jewish inferiority complex be exorcised and self-erected ghetto walls razed. But this objective calls for the establishment of Jewish community organizations in all important centers of Jewish population.

Ghettophobia is a pathological symptom. It is a disguised wish, born of burdens, to terminate Jewish life. It objects to meaningful Jewish survival programs—not out of fear that the effort may fail—but out of fear that it may succeed. Whenever Jews repudiate such programs on the ground that they are too Jewish, they betray a disguised suicidal wish. There is no arguing against such a psychopathic fear. Only those who do not suffer from self-hatred are in a position to revolutionize Jewish life. They alone may overcome the internal and external obstacles to creative survival which personal and institutional individualism has imposed.

2.   JUDAISM'S CONTRIBUTION TO AMERICAN LIFE

American Jews who substitute the concept of exemplary people for the supernaturalist version of Chosen People should strive to exemplify the ideals and practices of ethical peoplehood. What constitutes ethical nationhood? In his landmark address at Honolulu before the American Bar Association, Senator J. W. Fulbright defined its antithesis as "The Great Society is a Sick Society." He said in part:

> Standing in the smoke and rubble of Detroit, a Negro veteran said: "I just got back from Vietnam a few months ago, but you know, I think the war is here."
>
> There are in fact two wars going on. One is the war of power politics which our soldiers are fighting in the jungles of Southeast Asia. The other is a war for America's soul which is being fought in the streets of Newark and Detroit and in the halls of Congress, in churches and protest meetings and on college campuses, and in the hearts and minds of silent Americans from Maine to Hawaii. I believe that the two wars have something to do with each other, not in the direct, tangibly casual way that bureaucrats require as proof of a connection between two things, but in a subtler moral and qualitative way that is no less real for being intangible. Each of these wars might well be going on in the absence of the other; but neither, I suspect, standing alone, would seem so hopeless and demoralizing.
>
> The connection between Vietnam and Detroit is in their conflicting and incompatible demands upon traditional American values. The one demands that they be set aside, the other that they be fulfilled. The one demands the acceptance by America of an imperial role in the world, or of what our policymakers like to call the "responsibilities of power," or of what I have called the "arrogance of power." The other demands freedom and social justice at home, an end to poverty, the fulfillment of our flawed democracy and an effort to create a role for ourselves in the world which is compatible with our traditional values. The question, it should be emphasized, is not whether it is *possible* to engage in traditional power politics abroad

and at the same time to perfect democracy at home, but whether it is possible for *us Americans*, with our particular history and national character, to combine morally incompatible roles. . . .

"It is excellent," wrote Shakespeare, "to have a giant's strength; but it is tyrannous to use it like a giant." By using our power like a giant, we are fostering a world environment which is, to put it mildly, uncongenial to our society. By our undisciplined use of physical power, we have divested ourselves of a greater power: the power of example. How can we commend peaceful compromise to the Arabs and the Israelis when we are unwilling to suspend our relentless bombing of North Vietnam? How can we commend democratic social reform to Latin America when Newark, Detroit, and Milwaukee are providing explosive evidence of our own inadequate efforts at democratic social reform? How can we commend the free enterprise system to Asians and Africans when in our own country it has produced vast, chaotic, noisy, dangerous, and dirty urban complexes while poisoning the very air and land and water? There may come a time when Americans will again be able to commend their country as an example to the world, and more in hope than confidence.

At the same time, our purposeless and undisciplined use of power is causing a profound controversy in our own society. This in a way is something to be proud of. We have sickened but not succumbed, and just as a healthy body fights disease, we are fighting the alien concept which is being thrust upon us, not by history but by our policymakers in the Department of State and the Pentagon. We are proving the strength of the American Dream by resisting the dream of an imperial destiny. We are demonstrating the validity of our traditional values by the difficulty we are having in betraying them.

Some years ago Archibald MacLeish characterized the American people as follows:

"Races didn't bother the Americans. They were something a lot better than any race. They were a People. They were the first self-constituted, self-declared, self-created People in the history of the world. And their manners were their own business. And so were their politics. And so, but ten times so, were their souls."

Now the possession of their souls is being challenged by the false and dangerous dream of an imperial destiny. It may be that the challenge will succeed, that America will succumb to becoming a traditional empire and will reign for a time over what must surely be a moral if not a physical wasteland, and then, like the great empires of the past, will decline or fall. Or it may be that the effort to create so grotesque an anachronism will go up in flames of nuclear holocaust. But if I had to bet my money on what is going to happen, I would bet on this younger generation —this generation of young men and women who reject the inhumanity of war in a poor and distant land, who reject the poverty and sham in their own country, who are telling their elders what their elders ought to have known—that the price of empire is America's soul and that the price is too high.

The spiritual dilemma in American life stems from the dichotomy between secular and spiritual education. That sharp division of educational functions has widened the gap between the secular and the spiritual interests of the American people. Secular interests, all too often, meet with fulfillment in total disregard of spiritual interests, while spiritual interests—when cultivated as tradition and unrelated to everyday interests— are regarded as unrealistic and irrelevant. The disparity between thought and action, theory and practice, is more pronounced when spiritual interests are cultivated in the key of traditional supernaturalism.

The failure to integrate spiritual with secular interests has corrupted contemporary civilization. Among the principal manifestations of moral erosion, Paul Goodman names "the military industrial combines, the perverted universities, the rubber stamp Congress, the brutal police, imperialist adventurers, hidden military governments, the immoral, unjust, and impolitic Vietnam war. . . ." (*Commentary*, June 1968).

In the Torah Jews have a potent instrument with which to humanize and civilize the human being, provided that it functions in life, not merely in thought. The Jewish tradition regards

Torah study as the holiest form of worship; and in the Rabbinic tradition Torah was considered most significant and essential to salvation. Jewish liturgy proclaims Torah study as "our life and length of our days" and a manifestation of God's love for Israel. Noting Jewish self-dedication to a life of Torah the followers of Mohammed called the Jews "the people of the book."

Transposed into the key of religious humanism, Torah study means the lifelong concern with spiritual interests—the first priority in the education of man and his salvation. Throughout the centuries during which Jews were segregated, Torah study provided them with the control and guidance necessary in meeting their moral and legal responsibilities. Now that Jews have been fully integrated into an open democratic society, they have to meet the legal and moral responsibilities of that society. The First Amendment, which prohibits the establishment of religion, places the responsibility upon all American citizens to utilize the insights of their own spiritual heritage in the discharge of their legal and moral duties.

Fortunately, the federal and state governments realize the importance of religious institutions and have in the course of time enacted legislation toward exempting church properties from taxation, the support of the chaplaincy program for the military services, and other privileges, all indicating respect for and approval of the services of religious institutions vis-à-vis the character education of our communities and citizenry.

But what proportion of our population is affiliated with or subject to the teachings of our religious institutions? Are we not encouraging in the growing generation distorted ideas about religion and a negative attitude toward it by eliminating from our elementary and secondary school curricula recognition of, and respect for, religious values as such? We must plan to enhance the prestige of mature religion by appropriate appreciation of its values. Is not the seeming lack of ethical standards in government agencies at all levels, in part at least, the result of our educational system which has eliminated instruction in the ethical values that are rooted in group religion? Such teachings must be made a part of the general curriculum without reference to particular dogma and without offending any established church.

We should resolve the spiritual dilemma inherent in a democracy like ours by recognizing the religion inherent in American civilization. American religion can and must be both universal and indigenous. Whatever religious teaching might then be incorporated into our public educational system or program would have universal reference. It would, on the one hand, refer to the historical cultural experience of mankind. It would propound the principles which apply to all peoples, nations and races of men and bring those principles within the range of sympathy and understanding of our young people. To be indigenous such American religion must have particularity, the particularity of the life, the strivings, the experience, the travails, the failures, the hopes and the ideals of the American people. The religion which is to guide us in our lives as Americans must derive from our experiences as a nation and its endeavors to achieve life abundant. It must be an indigenously American religion.

Let not the bogeymen of past history—the national fanaticism of totalitarian states, the ambition for control and subjugation of multitudes by power driven leaders—incapacitate our better judgment and discriminatory faculties. A nation that is animated by an ethically religious fervor need not be totalitarian, chauvinistic or egomaniac. Is not the very fact that nationhood is capable of becoming so menacing a most compelling reason for bringing it under the control of ethical motivation? There is much sense in the well-known retort to the fling at religion as being merely a pirate's affair: "Who so needs religion as do pirates?"

The religion that is indispensable to the life of a democratic nation cannot be one that would sanction any tendency either to isolationism or to imperialism, to the suppression of the freedom of its citizens or to the repudiation of international law and responsibility. On the contrary, by the same token that we must discriminate between democratic and totalitarian nationhood, we must also discriminate between ethical and jingoistic religion. Ethical religion, far from suborning the crimes of nationhood, could act as a powerful deterrent to those tendencies.

It should not be difficult to determine which spiritual values of ethical religion must be stressed in our national life now. All that is necessary is to identify those dangerous tendencies which are most flagrant and most urgently in need of being countered by spiritual efforts and resources. It will suffice to indicate three such tendencies.

One dangerous tendency which must be checked is predominantly intellectual in character. Due to the tremendous strides of the sciences, the human mind is apt to require the habit of reducing realities, events and situations to terms lower than those in which they actually function in human life. This habit has proved fruitful in scientific research. When generalized and applied in the field of human values, it becomes a kind of disease known as "reductionism" or "scientism." Although values are determined partly by facts, the two are mutually heterogeneous.

Unfortunately "reductionism" is not confined to scientists. The man on the street spouts that jargon to emancipate himself from the sense of duty and responsibility. The new deities are cause and effect and the other scientific categories which help us to understand the physical world. The realization of the part played by heredity, environment and circumstances in determining the character and conduct of human beings, and particularly the role of the unconscious through the science of psychoanalysis, compels us to reorient ourselves in our world outlook. Thus, if we carry the methods of biology and sociology into the field of human values and treat human responsibility, on an international as well as on a personal scale, as an anachronism, we undermine the very foundations of human society.

To counteract that tendency we must draw upon an intuition which the historical religions stress, each in its own way, when they affirm that there is more to reality, especially to human reality, than can possibly be reduced to scientific formulation. That "more" or "plus" is the operation of a cosmic power that controls and directs our strivings to satisfy our biological and psycho-social needs. Because of its unexpected and unforseeable character, and its irreducibility to those biological and psycho-social factors, we may rightly regard it as spiritual or as transcending our empirical needs. By cultivating in the growing generation the wisdom to associate that cosmic power with the ethical urge and the sense of moral responsibility, we would lay the foundation of high character in the minds and hearts of our citizenry. We would thus forestall the danger of automatism or robotism. *If we want our nation to consist of free and self-determining persons, we dare not withhold from our children this awareness of the creative and the transcendent which men have always reckoned with whenever they affirmed the existence of an ethical and spiritual Deity.*

A second tendency in the life of democratic nations which is likely to wreak destruction, unless properly channeled, is predominantly emotional in character. That is the emphasis which the modern nation places upon the loyalty of its citizens, an emphasis which implies that loyalty be supreme. Little did Josiah Royce, the great American philosopher of idealism, dream that the ideal of loyalty, which he regarded as the main source of all moral and religious values, would in our generation be so corrupted as to be employed in behalf of the most brutal and bloody assault on humanity. Yet the fact remains that despite the vast holocaust of millions of human beings which the perversion of loyalty to state and nation has entailed, not even the democratic nations have grown any less monopolistic in their claim upon the loyalty of the individual citizen.

The growing complexity of the world economy and the progressive intricacy of the world's political affairs make it necessary for human beings to act in mass. It has become imperative for the individual to conform, to keep in step. If the democratic nations do not wish to be transformed into societies like those perfected by the ants and the bees, if they realize that their survival and growth in mind and spirit depend on the amount of latitude and freedom allowed the individual citizen, they must keep alive in their civilizations and foster in their educational systems the basic truth which the historic religions at their best have sought to emphasize: *that each human being is a unique, non-repeatable and unexpendable entity, a world in himself as well as a means to both nation and mankind.* Any social or political system which disregards this truth is bound to destroy in the individual that human differentia which the historic religions regard as the image of God.

The third tendency in the life of a democratic nation which needs the control of a religious ideal is "rugged individualism." This is the opposite pole to the danger of liquidating individuality. Adam Smith's economic philosophy and the individualism of the nineteenth century assumed that everybody's genuine interests would be served if everybody were permitted to follow the lead of his enlightened self-interest. Experience has proved that this free-for-all scramble is only a pseudo-democracy. To counteract this, a modern nation must be imbued with the ideal of justice, as the great prophets of Israel envisaged it. The soul of justice is equality which, as an ethical concept, is the right of every human being to all the available opportunities to bring to fruition whatever potentiality for good he possesses. In the Declaration of Independence all men are said to have been created equal. Both the language and the sentiment are taken from the Judeo-Christian tradition. The concept of creation reminds us of the transcendent factor that constitutes the human differentia. Applied to the concept of equality, it reminds us that *equality derives its validation not from experience or expediency but from the spiritual source to which we trace the human differentia.*

In *The American Dilemma* Gunnar Myrdal reveals the chasm that divides our profession of equality from the practice of it. He points out that the greatness of the ideal has become the occasion for our cynical rationalizations to cover our guilt feelings. It is not enough to distill our ideals from our religious traditions. We must integrate them into the habits of living and thinking by incorporating them into legislation, mores and educational content. We must realize that a *democracy should be religionized through its institutions.* We must practice what we profess.

The struggle, for example, of the Negroes for equality of opportunities with the rights to engage in the pursuit of life, liberty and happiness is one that involves moral issues which unless dealt with forthwith in a spirit of justice may shatter the very life of the American nation. According to Joseph C. Hough, Jr., it "represents a demand for a new stance toward whites, and a new appreciation of being black. It is a call for self-determination, equal opportunity, and full appreciation for black men in a white man's nation."

As long as the Negroes under the leadership of the martyred Dr. Martin Luther King and other moderates confined their protests to sit-ins, marches and passive resistance, the majority of Jews supported their struggle. But when the tocsin of Black Power was sounded and American cities, schools and universities became the battleground for abrasive confrontation and violence, liberal Americans—who recognized the gravity of Negro grievances, yet deplored their methods—faced a dilemma. Liberal Jews were further baffled, if not alienated, by the intrusion of virulent anti-Semitism into the liturgy of the Black Panthers and their new left allies.

Although there are no easy nor instant solutions, general guidelines in the application of Jewish experience to the current crisis in race and human relations may be indicated. The Negro is struggling to evolve and safeguard his identity in white America. He is at the starting line of the long, hard road which the Jew has trod throughout the ages. Only after the Negro shall have achieved cultural autonomy, full equality and self-respect will he be able to live authentically in two civilizations. After two thousand years of experience—in segregated ghettos and in open societies—Jews have not wholly mastered that art.

Granted that the blacks reject a teach-in on how the Jewish people survived persecution and on how they are trying to cope with freedom, yet Jews should understand more profoundly than others the need of Afro-Americans to achieve their own authentic life-style. With understanding will come forbearance and helpfulness. Ultimately the blacks may turn to the Jewish community for counsel and help in building a better America. The Jewish response would then express the role of Torah in American life.

What differentiates an indigenous religion from the universal is its distinctive sancta, rites and ceremonies. The United States of America has been developing and accumulating the religious sancta, the heroes, documents, texts, places, events and all other foci of collective interest which are regarded as representative of the needs of the people to fulfill its destiny and the needs of the individual for the good of his soul. The *Freedom Train* which traveled from state to state carrying the most valued documents of American national life was like a sacred Ark carrying the Torah of the United States. It is no exaggeration to call these documents sacred and to characterize the expedition as religious. By what logic can we deny the description of "holy" to those hymns, our national anthems, the spiritual stimulation of our national solidarity?

Our American history abounds in heroes, those who created and maintained our nation and those whose minds and spirits contributed to our great cultural and moral wealth. Many places at home and abroad have been sanctified by blood and tears. Our calendar has many dates dedicated to highly cherished ideals. We have enough annals, laws and prophesies, psalms and wisdom literature worthy of being canonized as Sacred Writ. These sancta should shine in their own light, radiating from the adventures, successes and frustrations of our American people struggling to achieve its own destiny of high ethical purpose. To shrink from taking the logical step of recognizing these native resources of the spirit as divine and as the substance of our emerging American religion is to waste energy of the highest order. Energy that is pent up or wasted avenges itself by becoming destructive. Considered as patriotism, that energy could be employed in the hate-ridden service of bigotries. All that is here proposed is not the *invention* of a new religion. It is a suggestion to *discover* for ourselves the valuable undercurrents of American life and to bring them up to wholesome fruition rather than permit them to run to waste.

If Jews are to be fully integrated into American life—without forfeiting their historical and contemporary identification with the Jewish people—they should make their own contribution to the realization of the American dream. That threefold contribution should embody a demythologized naturalistic conception of

God, the power of conscience rather than the consciousness of power, and devotion to the national ideal of life, liberty and the pursuit of happiness unmarred by self-seeking greed.

In its publication *The Faith of America* the Reconstructionist Foundation has formulated a religious version of the American Dream. If religion is to influence the life of a nation, it must be indigenous thereto. It must celebrate the events, places, heroes and the writings that have significance in the collective consciousness of a people.

National holidays call attention to the institutions and ideals that the nation holds sacred. As a rule, the observance of these days is perfunctory and mainly recreational. Their deeper meaning rarely emerges from the hard shell of shallow patriotism in which it is encased. But these holidays can attain spiritual significance if they are regarded in terms of a national religion and associated with the formative ideals of the American conscience. The following national holidays illustrate this association:

1. *New Year's Day:* for rededication to American ideals. The beginning of a new year offers occasion to take spiritual inventory of where the nation stands with respect to the fulfillment of its traditions and to renewal of devotion to its highest purposes.

2. *Lincoln's Birthday:* for devotion to the ideals of equality and fraternity. The humanity of Abraham Lincoln—who in the midst of Civil War expressed charity toward all, malice toward none—transcended racial, religious and sectional differences. His emancipation of the slaves should remind America of its unfinished business in giving political, economic and social opportunity to their descendants.

3. *Washington's Birthday:* for rededication to the responsibilities of nationhood. Since Washington presided at the birth of the nation with its promise of a better way of life, his anniversary should invite reflection on what the nation should mean to Americans and to mankind.

4. *Arbor Day:* for the conservaton of all natural resources. Inaugurated to halt the despoliation of forests and to replant them, Arbor Day should encompass the entire American en-

vironment. Unless the depredations of undirected technology and unrestricted industry are controlled, America will disturb the balance of nature and endanger its own survival. In the words of David Brower, former executive director of the country's most militant conservation group: "Looking at the whole earth as one ecosphere, we want to work hard toward restoring it and preserving it. We cannot go on fiddling while the earth's wild places burn in the fires of our undisciplined technology" (*The New York Times*, May 4, 1969).

5. *Memorial Day:* The solemn remembrance of those who gave their lives for their country should inspire citizens to make the nation worthy of such sacrifice.

6. *Flag Day:* Reverence for the flag is a form of idolatry unless it symbolizes loyalty to American democratic ideals and institutions. The pledge of allegiance should invoke the values that inhere in the American way of life and the privilege of sharing in it.

7. *Independence Day:* for reflection on the uses of freedom. All freedom involves responsibility toward one's own people and includes all mankind.

8. *Labor Day:* Through labor man helps to create his own world and to affect the destiny of the human race. But the dignity of labor depends upon its free and voluntary character as well as the adequacy of its compensation in providing for the needs of the laborer and his family.

9. *Constitution Day:* The United States is a government of laws, not of men. The importance of the Constitution does not rest alone on its specific provisions, but on its underlying principle. That principle defines and limits governmental authority and the responsibilities of citizens. Constitution Day should inspire Americans to continue translating into law the ideals of justice and righteousness.

10. *Columbus Day:* Columbus' daring attempt to reach the East by traveling west opened up a new continent. He was followed by a host of intrepid explorers and pioneers whose self-reliance and adventure has become a characteristic element of the American tradition. The observance of Columbus Day

should keep alive that spirit and stimulate the continuing search for ever-better ways of living.

11. *United Nations Day:* for rededication to world cooperation and peace. National sovereignty does not mean national ir-responsibility. In a world of closely knit economic and cultural ties, no nation can live in isolation; all are interdependent. All must learn to work together to their mutual advantage and for the welfare of all people everywhere. United Nations Day should serve as an occasion for renewing the American commit-ment to its ideals as well as to progressive amendment in keep-ing with changing times and with its own changing nature and functions.

12. *Election Day:* The exercise of suffrage is a sacred right and responsibility. Election Day should make the citizen aware of his share in government. He should cast his ballot conscientiously, placing the public welfare, as he sees it, above considerations of personal, sectional or partisan gain.

13. *Thanksgiving Day:* A blessing not appreciated is easily lost. Americans should not take for granted the blessings of living in a land of almost boundless opportunities without giving thought to the moral foundation on which that welfare rests. Thanksgiving should deepen awareness of those moral founda-tions and of human dependence upon the reciprocal responsibility of men and nations, which is the manifestation of Divinity.

What will then become of the historical religions? Those which claim to be based on supernatural revelation, having as their goal the immortality or otherworldly salvation of their communicants, have no competition to fear. What they offer lies outside the scope of American religion. Nor need there be concern among those historical religions which reinterpret the traditional miracles and concepts of salvation. Insofar as these religious groups carry with them the great historic civilizations, they perform the valuable service of broadening the mental and spiritual horizons of the individual American citizen. All the historical religions are leavening agencies in the American civilization and have the important role of emphasizing those religious elements which could help the religion of America to become a force for world unity as well as the solidarity of its own people. They could prevent the religion of America from degenerating into expression of national megalomania and an instrument of heresy hunting.

All of this implies that it is possible to be an adherent of more than one religion. The sense in which we have used the term "religion"—a way of life based on spiritual values—does not limit it to any particular method of validation or any exclusive method of salvation. There is nothing intellectually untenable or morally wrong with living in two civilizations and accepting the religious values in which each of them articulates its highest aspirations. It has been aptly stated that we are unable to serve two masters, but only when one of them is Mammon.

The various historic religions professed by Americans would, in addition to whatever religious traditions and values they sponsor, be in a position to stress the values necessary to help the religion inherent in American life to emerge. Americans, becoming more conscious of religious values, enunciated generally in schools and practiced admittedly by government agencies, will be less self-conscious about, and more attentive to, their own historic religious affiliations.

When the founders of the United States introduced the First Amendment to the Constitution they were moved by the history they had experienced in Europe: the power and influence of organized religion in governments and vice versa, and the political and religious domination imposed on citizenry. These were the tyrannies from which they had fled and from which they wished to protect themselves and their posterity in the new nation they were building. To them separation of church and state meant eliminating any possibility of either church or state becoming involved in power politics vis-à-vis one another. The danger still exists. But if the adherents of organized religions, especially their leaders, will restrain themselves, and if all Americans will keep aware of their privileges and ethical responsibilities as citizens, there will be no jockeying for positions of authority in favor of, or against, any religious institution or teaching.

CHAPTER VIII*

The Problem of Jewish
Education in the Diaspora

1. THE COMMUNAL RESPONSIBILITY FOR JEWISH EDUCATION

JEWISH education in the diaspora poses the following problems: (1) What kind of agency should administer the
transmission of the social and spiritual heritage of the Jewish
people from generation to generation? (2) How shall that agency
stimulate the demand for Jewish education as well as create the
means to meet that demand?

Under ancient conditions of human society parents assumed
the responsibility for the transmission of their peoples' heritage,
although they might delegate that function to the teacher or
school. Among the Jews during the latter half of the Second
Commonwealth era, parental responsibility for Jewish education was shared by the nation. The statement in the treatise
Nedarim 81a, "Be sure to make provision for the education of
the children of the poor, for they may become a source of
Torah knowledge," reflects an institutionalized outlook on the
part of Jews with a strong sense of national self-awareness. No
other nation had attained so sensitive an awareness of how
indispensable the transmission of the social and spiritual heritage
was to its continued existence. Only the Jewish people could
say of its tradition that it was an inheritance of the entire
people (Deut. 33:4). Now that modern secular nations have

*Condensed from *Judaism in Transition*.

adopted the foregoing educational policy, the transmission of a national heritage has come to be universally compulsory.

What has been the situation in Jewish life which, for the last nineteen hundred years, has not had any national state to enforce its will? Until its emancipation from medieval disabilities, the Jewish nation in exile consisted of communities that exercised considerable social autonomy and had the power to enforce their will almost as effectively as the governments of their host nations. There were no complicated problems of administration, and the Jews managed to attain, as a rule, a higher level of literacy than their surrounding populations. During the hundred years prior to World War II the Jewish communities of Central Europe were granted, together with the alleviation of medieval disabilities, religious and educational autonomy. It was in Central Europe—rather than in the East European countries where the old type of Jewish learning prevailed—that modern Jewish scholarship arose.

In the United States, where the separation of the state and church was not conducive to the formation of organic Jewish communities, Jewish education suffered a great setback and Jewish illiteracy among first- and second-generation Jews made great strides. Manual workers who were drawn into unionism and socialism did not give their children any Jewish education. The rising Jewish middle class tried to discharge their responsibility for the Jewish education of their children by turning them over to "*siddur* peddlers" or by sending them to self-appointed, untrained teachers. The latter organized their own private *hedarim* (schools) which were usually conducted in ill-ventilated, ill-lighted rooms in crowded tenements. Those teachers as a rule had no knowledge of class pedagogy. With their retail method of teaching each child separately and sending him off when he was through with his individual recitation, they succeeded in developing, particularly in the brightest children, an ineradicable disgust for Judaism. The children of the very poor, who could not afford to pay tuition fees, were far better off than these *heder* victims. They attended Talmud Torah schools that were maintained by societies whose members contributed to their support. These schools were housed in buildings of their own and were manned by a better type of teachers. They were directed by a principal and followed an organized curriculum.

The Kehillah Experiment

Between 1910 and 1920—when metropolitan New York already had the largest urban aggregation of Jews in the world—a new development, the *Kehillah* movement, if encouraged, might have made New York Jewry as Jewishly productive as were Old World cities like Vilna, Warsaw or Odessa. That movement was sparked by an anti-Semitic remark made by the then Commissioner of Police to the effect that the Jewish population of the city had a larger criminal element in proportion to its numbers than the other immigrant populations. It was then that Dr. Judah Magnes rallied some of the wealthy uptown Jews and a greater number of the downtown poorer class in answer to his call for the formation of a *Kehillah*, or organic Jewish community. He hoped to bring together under one aegis all religious, educational, economic and social service activities whose coordination would create a sense of Jewish unity and solidarity.

Initially, the rich and well-born helped Dr. Magnes in the organization of the *Kehillah*. But they robbed it of its democratic character by making it the tail to the kite of the American Jewish Committee. The only creative institution which survived the demise of the *Kehillah* was its Bureau of Jewish Education, which became a beneficiary of the New York Federation of Philanthropies. Endowed with a million dollars by a Catholic, Burke, it was reorganized in 1940 under the name of The Jewish Education Committee of New York City. In a number of cities additional bureaus of Jewish education have been organized and maintained by the local Federations or Welfare Funds, which, for the most part, administer philanthropy for the poor. There is something psychologically vitiating in having Jewish education included among philanthropic activities. With the exception of New York City and one or two other city bureaus, neither their number nor their effectiveness scratched the surface of the Jewish educational problem. Hence public-spirited Jews organized the American Association for Jewish Education for the purpose of strengthening existing bureaus and creating new ones.

The significant fact about the organization of these bureaus of education is that it did not just happen, like the British Empire, in a fit of absent-mindedness. It all started (as did the resurrection of Hebrew, or the establishment of the State of Israel) as an idea of one Jew who envisaged the restoration of the Jewish people to creative life. It was Dr. Samson Benderly who proposed that Jewish education be a communal rather than solely parental responsibility. Dr. Benderly was a descendent of a Safed family that had migrated more than two centuries ago from a town in Turkey by the name of Benderly. From Safed he went to Beirut to study medicine and thence to Baltimore, where he practiced medicine under the tutelage of Dr. Harry Friedenwald who was the first president of the Zionist Organization of America. But possessed by a passionate desire to save Jewish life from disintegration, Benderly gave up his medical career. He established the first Hebrew-speaking school in the Western Hemisphere using the *Ivrit b'Ivrit* method then devised by the late David Yellin of Jerusalem.

When Dr. Benderly learned of Dr. Magnes' plan to create the *Kehillah* in New York, he unfolded his conception of Jewish education as no less a communal than a parental responsibility. The parents might delegate to others the function of educating their children as Jews. It was the function of the community however to create schools, to supervise them, to train teachers, to establish standards, plan curricula and conduct all other educational activities in a well-organized civic community. What more important activity, then, for the nascent *Kehillah* than that of creating a department of education to be administered by a bureau and its staff?

By now it seems self-evident that the Jewish community should administer Jewish education for all the Jewish parents. But sixty years ago that was a radical and revolutionary idea. Thanks to the charm and persuasiveness of Dr. Magnes, and to the findings of a study made of the Jewish educational situation, Jacob H. Schiff donated funds to establish the first communal bureau of Jewish education. It is noteworthy that Magnes and Benderly—as well as Israel Friedlander, who was mainly responsible for bringing them together—were all Ahad Ha-Am Zionists. Their conception of communal responsibility for administering Jewish education was the logical consequence of Ahad Ha-Am's philosophy of Zionism which exhorted diaspora Jewry to recover its sense of peoplehood as a prerequisite for the return to *Eretz Yisrael.*

Had not the *Kehillah* been undermined by the Orthodox rabbinic contingent and had not a new movement offered to provide Jewish education in a more personal fashion and on easier terms than those which a community could offer, the Jewish social and spiritual heritage might have struck deeper roots in the life and character of the Jew, and Jewish illiteracy might have been averted. Paradoxical as it may seem, the successful competitor for the function of transmitting the Jewish heritage came to be the synagogue. It was the synagogue that offered to sell Jewish education more cheaply and on easier terms, such as standards, hours of attendance, and number of years required for graduation.

Effect of Congregationalism on Education

A highly important factor in moral and spiritual education is the auspices under which it is conducted. It makes all the difference in the world, as far as influencing the student's character and sense of values is concerned, whether the education in a way of life represents the will of God, of parents, of a congregation, of a nation or of a combination of some or of all of those authorities. The Jewish congregation in the United States is a new and unprecedented social entity. In the main it is a religious family club of homogeneously middle-class Jews—with Jewish intellectuals in short supply. Structurally, Jewish congregations are replicas of Protestant churches of the Congregational sects, with this important difference: The dominant motive in these churches is the identification of the parents with a particular theology or religious doctrine; the dominant motive in a Jewish congregation is the parents' desire to have their children accept their identification as Jews. For that purpose most American Jewish parents unconsciously live up to a principle which anthropology proves to be universal among all religions. That principle is that the content and spirit of a people's social heritage should be transmitted through the ritual of initiation. In other words, the *raison d'être* of an American Jewish congregation has hitherto been the wishes of the parents to have their children "Bar-Mitzvahed" or confirmed.

Thus the movement inaugurated by the *Kehillah* to bring Jewish education under communal auspices failed, and its functions were preempted by the synagogue. The United Synagogue, a third denominational organization of congregations which came to be known as Conservative, took its place alongside the strongly Reform Union of American Hebrew Congregations and the weaker Orthodox Union of Congregations. The top functionaires of the Conservative movement competed with the communal Talmud Torah schools for the opportunity of giving the children of American Jewish parents a Jewish education. As in economic, so also in spiritual competition, unfair tactics are resorted to. The communal movement for Jewish education was charged with being secular in spirit. Only the synagogue, it was claimed, was qualified to preserve the religious character of Jewish education. As a result, Jewish education fell between two stools: the communal school, which began to dwindle, and the congregational schools, which became Bar-Mitzvah factories.

In recent years the rabbis who can no longer condone the deterioration of Jewish education have initiated collective action to establish minimal requirements for Bar Mitzvah or confirmation. But the elevation of standards has not changed the attitude of parents whose Jewish illiteracy has not been reduced. Jewish education and spiritual life is like Mark Twain's description of the Platte River: "a mile wide and an inch deep."

All Jewish educational activities in the diaspora must be integrated in a cooperative undertaking based on the assumption that Jewish unity and solidarity will henceforth have to be compatible with diversity of world outlook. Educational machinery must not be confined to purely mechanical functions, such as helping schools with their fiscal and administrative problems, or teachers with their status and tenure. The corollary —non-interference with educational policy—would defeat the main purpose of Jewish education and fortify the separatist and divisive tendencies of existing denominations and sects. It would convert Jewish education into indoctrination for sectarian power and prestige.

The main purpose of all Jewish schools is to stress those values of the Jewish heritage which serve as a bond of unity and brotherhood. These values may be classified as follows: (1) The three-thousand-year history of Israel; (2) *Eretz Yisrael* as its common and continuous aspiration; (3) a vast literature recording Jewish spiritual life; (4) Hebrew as the original and resurrected vernacular of the Jewish people; (5) the Messianic goal of a warless world united by the will to social justice and ethical nationhood; (6) faith in the spiritual or transcendental meaning of human life; and (7) the Jewish calendar with its Sabbaths and festivals as dedicated to the activation of all the values inherent in the six foregoing items.

Both congregational and communal administration of Jewish educational activities need an orientation that transcends them both. The orientation of Jewish peoplehood makes Jewish people as a whole the logical and psychological source of Jewish educational administration. Hence the *de jure* existence of an identifiable Jewish people is required to underpin the education of posterity.

Jewish education is the first and most indispensable means for the achievement of the transmission of the social and spiritual Jewish heritage and for rendering it relevant to contemporary Jewish life. The Jewish people or world Jewry, represented by a Ministry for Jewish Education, should administer educational activities through bureaus in the diaspora. The Ministry itself should include Israeli educators on its staff, in order to insure free interchange of experience between Israel and the diaspora. A Hebrew Teachers College for the training of students from the diaspora should be established under the auspices of the Hebrew University.

The World Ministry for Jewish Education should (1) create a genuine demand on the part of parents for the most effective ways and means of transmitting the Jewish moral and spiritual heritage, and (2) provide ways and means to meet the demand.

As long as parents feel that a Jewish education places an unnecessary burden upon their children, no amount of improvement in the physical or pedagogic conditions can upgrade the educational situation. It may remain static, but it will not catch up with the growth of the Jewish population. A World Ministry of Jewish Education should reawaken in the hearts of parents something of that high worth which their ancestors attached to Jewish learning.

The initial effort should be directed toward the Jewish intellectual élite who create public opinion and determine a hierarchy of values for the less sophisticated. The intellectual élite will respond to the interpretation of Judaism as an evolving religious civilization, on the threshold of a new stage in its evolution.

More Study, Less Praying

In stimulating a demand for a Jewish education, most parents must be reached through their congregations and rabbis. Most American rabbis have become convinced that they can transform Jewish life only by renewing the ancient Rabbinic emphasis on Torah study. Throughout the Written and Oral Tradition the study of Torah is regarded as of far higher spiritual rank than worship and prayer. Whereas worship and prayer are directed toward the attainment of peace of mind, the study of Torah can set in motion all the moral influences that go into the molding of character and the shaping of society. Hence Torah study is stressed again and again as directly commanded by God; the duty of prayer is treated, on the whole, as a Rabbinic ordinance.

Jews assembling in the synagogue should gain some knowledge of their tradition and the application of that knowledge to their higher needs. As it is, they come mainly for the sermon, enjoy the music when it is good and tolerate the prayers and the Torah reading. Although a good sermon instructs, it carries no connection with the preceding one nor with the one following.

A sermon violates the rules of pedagogy, chiefly because the preacher stands three or four feet above contradiction and discussion.

Synagogue attendance should afford Jews the opportunity to grow in the knowledge and appreciation of their great and inexhaustible tradition. To be sure, it would mean that the rabbis would transform the synagogue into a *bet ha-midrash*, a house of study. Is not that in keeping with the unanimous teaching of our ancient Sages who recommended such a transformation? This transformation of the synagogue into a house of study would stimulate parents to demand a meaningful Jewish education for their children. It would enrich their own lives.

There are other than synagogue auspices under which Jews assemble from time to time. These include hundreds of Jewish communal centers, fraternal orders, such as B'nai B'rith which conducts Hillel Houses on college campuses. Many national women's organizations—Hadassah, Council of Jewish Women, sisterhoods, set aside time for Jewish study. These organizations publish books and periodicals containing educational material. But their efforts are sporadic and unsystematic. A World Jewish Ministry for education should prod the congregations, communal centers and the fraternal and service organizations to conduct their adult study courses in a spirit of dedication and systematic concentration. Many Jewish intellectuals could be enlisted in the kind of Jewish self-educational and reeducational campaign which a World Ministry for Jewish Education might conduct through the synagogue, the communal centers and fraternal and social service organizations. *All such efforts should aim at fostering in the adult Jewish population a passionate desire to transmit the Jewish heritage to their children.*

The organization of subject matter to translate the Jewish heritage into the modern universe of discourse will revive and enhance Jewish self-awareness. Otherwise it remains part of antiquity which is of interest mainly to archaeologists. The variegated content of that heritage should be organized into the familiar categories of Jewish history, religion, ethics, Hebrew language and literature, and into the much needed new category of Jewish civics. The preparation of such material in tractable form is a basic requirement. Even the Great Books Study Movement would not have progressed without the special publication of the texts to be studied and a guide like the Syntopicon which enables both students and teachers to use those texts to maximum advantage.

The preparation of such texts for Jewish subject matter is a far more complicated process than was involved in the preparation of the Great Books series. The classic heritage is, in its original form, cast into subject matter of different categories, whereas our own heritage, being part of the oriental universe of discourse, lacks that kind of division into categories. Moreover, on the principle of unity in diversity, the content of the Bible will yield different subject matter, when treated according to three such different versions as those of Samson Raphael Hirsch, Yehezkel Kaufmann and M. D. Cassuto. There must henceforth be room for all three versions in Jewish education, with freedom of each Jew to adopt whichever appeals most to him. But there must also be an awareness of a common denominator in all those versions, if they are to contribute to the creative self-awareness of the Jewish people.

Additional Functions of a World Ministry for Jewish Education

The category of Jewish civics is missing from Jewish education because Jewish scholars have shown little appreciation for the role of social structure in Jewish life. Thanks to the neglect of Jewish civics, there is a very ominous division of opinion concerning the future of diaspora Jewry and the relationship of Israel to diaspora Jewry. The rise of congregationalism should not have given rise to denominationalism, which is undermining the solidarity of the Jewish people. Lacking a definition of their Jewish civic status, Jews lack criteria for an authoritative definition of the very term "Jew." Jews have failed to realize to what extent social status is an important factor in a person's moral and spiritual life.

Additional activities which should occupy a World Ministry for Jewish Education with its affiliated local bureaus are:

To canvass college campuses for young men and women who might teach in Jewish schools while pursuing their graduate studies. Likewise to canvass the rabbinical seminaries for students who might prefer careers in Jewish education rather than the rabbinate. Such students should be guided and encouraged in their Jewish studies.

To stimulate the organization of Jewish high school classes which should be synchronized with the attendance of their students at public high schools, and to encourage their graduates to take up some career of Jewish service, particularly in Jewish education or the rabbinate.

To set up standards for graduation from elementary and secondary Jewish schools.

To obtain scholarships for children of parents who cannot afford to pay for the Jewish education of their children.

To set up standards for teacher employment in terms of salaries, vacations, pensions, and so on.

To summarize: The specific activities in which a World Ministry for Jewish Education would have to engage may be divided into two categories: first, those which aim to imbue the parents with such appreciation of their Jewish heritage as to arouse in them a genuine demand for help to transmit it to their children; second, to supply the most effective means and the most favorable conditions necessary to get the children to make that heritage part of their Jewish self-awareness. Thus once again can Jewish education perform the role of the historic Covenant which binds Jews into one followship and that fellowship to God: "This shall be My Covenant with them, said the Eternal, My spirit which is upon you, and the words which I have put into your mouth shall never depart from your mouth, nor from the mouth of your descendants, nor from the mouth of their descendants" (Isa. 59:21).

2. NEW EMPHASES IN JEWISH EDUCATION

Tradition is usually defined as the body of usages and beliefs transmitted from generation to generation. This definition, though true, does not give the slightest hint of the extent to which tradition has functioned as a civilizing agency in the evolution of mankind; it takes no note of the fact that the generations which transmit and the generations which receive the traditional usages and beliefs belong to the same social grouping, such as clan, tribe, nation, people or church. It ignores the role of tradition in arousing in members of the group an awareness of the group as a social unit, whose life extends both into the past and into the future and embraces the dead, the living and the unborn.

This awareness of the group transforms the life of the individual from a solitary and purposeless existence into a highly conscious striving to surmount his physical limitations. The stories which the poets narrate, the laws which the elders and the judges quote, the wisdom which the sages teach and the customs and folkways which the people observe enlarge the mental horizon of the individual. They extend the scope of his desires and interests to the furthest limits of the society to which he belongs. Through them he identifies himself with the generations of his people that preceded his birth, with those that will live after his death and with kinsmen, compatriots or coreligionists whom he has never seen and never expects to meet.

Thus, through tradition, man acquires a sense of social responsibility which reaches out beyond the immediate members of his family. From its original meaning the recognition of kinship, or kindness, has come to denote the sympathy extended toward all members of one's people. Through the same medium man learns the meaning of loyalty, which impels him to give priority to the welfare of the group over his own.

Since it is tradition that elicits such traits as loyalty and social responsibility, it is folly to dispense with it in education for character development. That is the error of those modernists who, in their eagerness to dissociate character education from training in obedience and conformity to traditional standards, deprecate all efforts at imparting specific religious education. Frequently parents who are in revolt against hidebound traditionalism declare: "I don't want my child to be indoctrinated. When he grows up, he will choose for himself what religious principles and practices, if any, he may feel to be important for him." But it is only through tradition that the child can learn the process of moral and spiritual evaluation. The individual's growth into mature and autonomous ethical personality is analogous to his growth in the power to use speech for purposes of self-expression. Parents do not delay the child's learning to speak until he can invent or choose a language of his own; they transmit their own vernacular to him. Why then deny him the knowledge of the standards of human society and of the prevailing ideas about life as a whole, which constitute the moral religious tradition? Even if children are not sent to religious schools, they are usually taught worthwhile ideals. But just as parents supplement the child's vernacular with systematic school training in grammar, rhetoric and literature, so they should supplement this vague, casual and more or less inarticulate imparting of higher ideals with a systematized presentation of them in the religious school.

Through the medium of his religious and moral tradition the child learns to recognize the group which is vitally concerned in his self-fulfillment as a human being. Most individuals identify themselves with a number of groups—political, economic or cultural—because of common interests. An American citizen may belong to his country, the capitalist class, the Order of Free Masons and an international sports organization. But not all these groups mean the same to him; not all contribute equally to his realization of the highest potentialities of his nature. It is important for him to recognize which group is vitally concerned in his efforts to attain the maximum harmonious fulfillment of his personal social desires and purposes. Such fulfillment is usually referred to as "salvation."

"Salvation" is not a popular concept because it has been associated with an otherworldly outlook that modern man has for the most part discarded. It need not, however, retain this connotation. The otherworldly churches taught that salvation could not be attained in this life but only after death. But the need for salvation survives all mistaken notions of it. The yearning for an autonomous and integrated personality motivates people who do not look forward to personal immortality; although they do not believe in a celestial paradise, they too are in quest of salvation.

Next to the sheltering solicitude of the home, the human being requires the social security of the larger fellowship to which the family unit belongs. Giving validity and status to the family, that fellowship conserves the family by regulating the sex relationship through ordinances and taboos. It stimulates the individual in his striving after personality in its most comprehensive sense. Its traditional ideals and standards imply certain expectations of its members whose attainment fills the individual with a deep satisfaction that makes an act of self-sacrifice a glorious experience. *That element of expectation which a fellowship expresses through its tradition is, therefore, among the most important creative influences on character.* Very few can forego the stimulus of that expectation.

For the Jew, tradition plays a unique role. Jews constitute a minority group which is always at a disadvantage. It is usually maligned, discriminated against and treated as the scapegoat for the sins of society in general. Harassed by external antagonism and a prey to mental anxiety and self-contempt, the Jew examines his behavior and that of his fellow Jews for some clue to the solution of the enigma. He adopts the protective coloring of Gentile manners and attitudes to blend into his environment. Or assuming a self-assertive truculence, he may flaunt his Jewishness to overcompensate for the hurt to his pride and self-respect. In his book *Juedischer Selbsthass* Theodore Lessing depicts the tragic lives of Jews who were ignorant of their tradition.

A tradition which would present in dignified fashion the case of the Jewish people is absolutely indispensable as a therapeutic to Jewish character. The Jew must regard Jewish life not through the eyes of a hostile civilization, but through the authentic voices of its own heroes, sages, poets, prophets and leaders. No civilization when viewed in the light of its own tradition can evoke feelings of disgust and revulsion. On the contrary, it preserves and transmits those aspects of life and thought which bind its posterity with the ties of love and loyalty. *Stifled by the poison gas of antipathy and contempt, the Jew requires the spiritual oxygen of his tradition to infuse his character with the therapy of human dignity.*

But while Jews cannot do without their tradition, they cannot do with that tradition as it has come down from the past. If tradition is to be a factor in the character training of the young, it must be modified to conform to scientific and rational human experience.

Tradition always pertains to a particular group. Its traditional beliefs are not abstract ideas, but specific doctrines about events, heroes and institutions which have played a part in the group's struggle for existence and, especially, against rival groups. Rivalries, which have long been dead, are recalled as a background for the heroic events and figures which give substance to the collective memory and incentive to courage and martyrdom. Before the period of the Enlightenment the Jewish tradition was transmitted as a counterclaim to Christianity and Mohammedanism, which had appropriated for their respective fellowships the title of the elect of God and the exclusive promise of salvation. Since Jewish tradition had always proclaimed that the Jews were the chosen of God, Judaism declared itself to be the only way to salvation. "All Israel will have a share in the world to come."

All this must now be changed. The value of Jewish tradition to the modern Jew is not dependent on its assertion of superiority over other traditions. Those traditions should not be considered its rivals, since they cannot function for the Jewish people, and the Jewish tradition cannot function for other peoples or fellowships. Jewish tradition should be transmitted as a cluster of human values existing in their own right. Anyone who keeps a diary would not like to see it destroyed, though it may not compare in literary and historical worth with that of Samuel Pepys. He values it because it is his own, because it reveals his own individuality. Whether good, bad or indifferent from a moralistic standpoint, the Jewish tradition—with its heroisms and events, its laws, struggles, tragedies, defeats, dreams and yearnings—constitutes the actual experiences of the people. Jews should want their children to weave these experiences into their own world, to appropriate them as an integral part of their own consciousness. Once communicated in this spirit, the Jewish tradition would fill a deep psychological need. The most obscure peoples find the drama of their history, the courage of their own heroes and the inspiration of their poets enough reason for cherishing their tradition. Apart from its relevance for Jews, the intrinsic worth of the Jewish tradition offers abundant reason for its cultivation.

The modern interpretation of the Jewish tradition should focus on universal loyalty and responsibility as a means of developing ethical character. "So be loyal to your own cause," wrote the philosopher Josiah Royce, "as thereby to serve the advancement of the cause of universal loyalty." Just as loyalty to one's own home expresses itself in protecting family life from corrupting and dinistegrating influences, so loyalty to one's fellowship and civilization should encompass all institutions that further human civilization and promote human welfare.

The Jewish tradition must be restated in terms of the scientific world outlook. As handed down from a pre-scientific era, that tradition is in conflict with scientific thought. Hence it is necessary to recognize as products of the popular imagination all those elements that cannot be maintained as historic fact. Artificial methods of interpretation which attempt to harmonize tradition with science are devious. Folklore and legend, properly understood, are the repositories of implied historical truth and fundamental values which have authenticity and permanent worth. The usages, which in the tradition are conceived as divine commandments, should be treated as human institutions, laws and mores intended to help man achieve salvation. The religious rites or observances should be treated as folkways which are associated with spiritual refinement and a poetic approach to reality.

No tradition can be effective so long as it is merely a way of speaking. It presupposes a functioning group life, a visible environment and other tangible evidence of collective activity. Hence the Jewish renaissance in Israel has become indispensable to the transmission of the Jewish tradition. In Israel the landscape is redolent of traditional associations and historic memories that awaken in the present generation a feeling of identity with the generations of the past. The calendar that regulates all the routines of the people's social and economic life takes cognizance of Sabbaths and festivals, of historical anniversaries and contemporary national events. Tradition is integrated into the daily life of the Jewish people as it cannot be integrated anywhere else. In America at Christmas the Christian tradition is all-pervasive and expresses itself in visual symbols, music and secular life. In Israel the Jewish tradition is no less pervasive. The mere consciousness of such a center of Jewish creativity and autonomy engenders in Jews everywhere an enhanced awareness of their collective being and of their identity with the historic tradition of their people.

But even more immediate evidence of collective Jewish life is essential if Jewish tradition is to function in the diaspora. Nothing less than large-scale communal life can make the Jewish child feel that Jewish tradition helps adjust him to his environment and contributes to his achievement of personality. The lack of a flourishing Jewish community life is a formidable obstacle that prevents Jewish education from meeting the need for character training. But it is not the only obstacle. The whole cultural heritage of the Jewish people must be freshly evaluated and suitable educational material to meet the needs of the child must be developed.

Let us take, for example, the Bible. As long as it was viewed as the word of God, its study was regarded as important. Its text was approached with awe, and the study of it was a *mitzvah* or religious rite calculated to win the favor of God. Hence parents and children felt the study of the sacred text to be a rewarding activity even though the words may have conveyed no significant meaning to the child's mind. But with our skepticism as to the traditional doctrine of revelation, and with our unanthropomorphic conception of God, the Bible can be used in education only on the basis of its intrinsic interest. But only the mature and well-informed adult who is capable of reconstructing in imagination the life situation recorded and commented upon in biblical literature can understand the Bible. For the child Bible study may not yield significant meaning on the basis of its intrinsic value alone.

The biblical books are but fragmentary expressions of the life that pulsed through the Jewish people during the biblical period of its history. The child, with his lack of experience and with his limited powers of inference, cannot piece together the fragments into a meaningful pattern. A scholarly adult standing among the ruins of the Acropolis can regale his spirit by reconstructing the city of Athens in the age of Pericles. But the average American schoolboy would see only the scattered and broken ruins of ancient temples. Even adults seldom read the Bible although they pay it lip reverence because they lack the background necessary for its proper appreciation. How then can we expect children to find its study interesting?

The same is true of the study of the prayer book. As long as prayer had a sacramental, quasi-magical significance, the mere utterance of prayers was felt to be of value in influencing God to favor the worshiper. But for modern man prayer has lost that meaning. The traditional prayers express archaic and anachronistic beliefs such as the doctrine of resurrection and the hope for the restoration of sacrificial worship. To be sure, an adult who studies the deeper psychological implications of the traditional prayers may find relevant thoughts and sentiments therein. But such ideas, even when restated in modern idiom, are usually beyond the comprehension of young children. In their traditional form they are usually meaningless to most adults.

As long as Jews believed the traditional version of Jewish history, the miracles with which it is replete held a certain fascination for the child. But his early scientific training soon leads him to ask: "Is this true?" If the answer is negative, or a qualified affirmative, the glamour of wonderland is dispelled. A confident affirmative will only postpone the issue until the young adolescent's independent reasoning leads him to conclude that all religious instruction was a product of hypocrisy and superstition.

All history, as a concatenation of causes and effects, is beyond the grasp of the immature mind. Jewish history is almost co-extensive in time with the history of human civilization and, in space, with the nations of the Near East, northern Africa, Europe and even America. It is so interwoven with the history of other peoples among whom the Jews have lived as an unassimilated minority that we must be able to follow the fortunes and destinies of these nations in order to understand the career of the Jewish people. The study of Jewish history therefore requires the knowledge and capacity for rational generalization which puts historic events into a wide and constantly changing perspective. This cannot be expected of children.

The Jewish school as a religious school implies that religion is the most important subject of instruction. But what is true of the material in the other subjects applies in even greater degree to religion. When it was the consensus that God had revealed to Israel, in the written and oral Torah, laws and rites to guide them, Torah study was regarded as indispensable to their welfare in this world and to their salvation in the world to come. This simple doctrine, uncomplicated by theories about God, could motivate children to learn Jewish religion. Such is no longer the case. With scientific skepticism challenging traditional theological doctrines, with disillusionment at the failure of religion to abolish war and poverty and with growing cynicism as to the capacity of human nature to respond to any but the most materialistic motives, the cultivation of a religious attitude demands a philosophic reinterpretation of the conception of God. Jews cannot indoctrinate their children with the theological creed of their fathers because children are quick to detect a lack of conviction on the part of parents and teachers. *And there is no educational material adapted for children to help them attain a mature conception of God which meets the challenge of modern thought.*

Lacking the motivating environment of an integrated Jewish community, and lacking educational material of intrinsic interest to the Jewish child, the concerned Jewish adult orbits in a vicious circle. In the absence of relevant Jewish educational material the Jewish curriculum is devoid of interest. The children's lack of interest "justifies" parents in withdrawing their children from schools and in withholding their moral and financial support. Their negativism discourages the creation of new educational material and techniques which might have served the present needs of the Jewish child. At what point can this vicious circle be broken?

Obviously not at the point of the child's participation in the educational process. The social situation is beyond his comprehension and the content of the Jewish instruction does not appeal to his present interest. Adults, however, are in a position to appreciate the new need for Jewish education. *Common sense indicates that the emphasis be put on the education of the Jewish adolescent and adult rather than on that of the child.* Not that Jews should discontinue their present effort to maintain and conduct schools for Jewish children. But they must recognize that no serious advance can be made in the Jewish education of their children unless and until they inaugurate an extensive movement for the Jewish education of the adult.

A well-planned and vigorously executed program for adult Jewish education would break through the vicious circle described above. Adults would want their children as well as themselves to possess the sort of Jewish knowledge that would make for self-respect. They would therefore encourage their children to take advantage of the best available facilities for Jewish instruction and would interest themselves in the effort to improve the quality of that instruction. Finally, they would experience the need for themselves and for their children of a functioning, status-conferring Jewish community, so that Jewish education would not be a thing detached and remote from all other vital interests, but would be integrated into the communal life of the Jewish people. And, having experienced this need, they would seek to satisfy it by helping to effect the necessary reorganization of American Jewry.

In this way Jewish education can be restored to the important place it once occupied in Jewish life. It can be made to bring mental healing to the Jew and to enhance his life. And it can do more. By stimulating a live interest in the development of ethical personality, it can tap a new source of social and spiritual energy that will contribute to the strength which mankind now needs in its struggle against the besetting forces of darkness and the menace of universal cataclysm.

3. THE RABBINIC TRAINING FOR OUR DAY

A rabbinic school should furnish its students with an extensive and intensive knowledge of the Jewish heritage, of human nature and of social conditions, and with the ability to synthesize that knowledge and to apply it to the specific situations with which they will have to deal as rabbis.

There are different ways of transmitting and cultivating the Jewish heritage. It is one thing to study Jewish history, language, philosophy and law as one studies the ancient civilizations of the Greeks and the Romans. It is quite a different thing to study these branches of Jewish knowledge as the civilization of a living and struggling people, with a view to revitalizing that civilization. The difference will express itself in the very organization of the subject matter, in the type of thing that will be emphasized and in a variety of indefinable ways which should differentiate an institution that trains rabbis from one that trains archeologists. The rabbinical institution must focus its attention on the present and not on the past. Its concern with the past should be dictated solely by the purpose of understanding the determining forces that do and that should operate in Jewish life today and of helping the rabbi to cope with the insistent Jewish problems of the present. The rabbinical institution which loses sight of that principle is bound to send forth either frustrated archeologists or half-baked rabbis.

The rabbinic training nowadays is called upon to meet a need which is entirely the outcome of present-day conditions. That is the need of fostering a sense of the living reality of the Jewish people and consciously developing the implications of such reality. In the American environment, where sharing the cultural life of the majority has for Jews become a matter of course, there is the danger that the Jewish people might assume the nature of a Platonic idea, without necessarily having its counterpart in tangible reality. In common with those Platonic ideas, the Jewish people is apt to be regarded as something perfect, finished, residing solely in "the mind of God"—or its equivalent, the literature regarded as divine—where it is free from the grossness of physical actuality. It is tempting to contemplate the Jewish people as a Church, and the more invisible the Church the better. For is not invisibility the very essence of the spiritual? Such a conception of the Jewish people simplifies matters and obviates the troublesome problem of adjustment. There is a certain esthetic pleasure in sentimentalizing occasionally about a remote ancestry. The very remoteness of ancestors is conducive to the tendency of idealizing and apotheosizing them into a race of supermen who knew God more truly and more intimately than any other people and who noted down their experiences in the Bible, which is the greatest religious classic of all time. It should be the purpose of a rabbinic training to forestall any such easy solution of the Jewish problem and to cultivate in the student a keen yearning for a Jewish life that is visible and tangible, that expresses itself in our present-day world as the interaction of a cooperative group of men, women and children who have practical interests and concrete social purposes in common.

To develop that yearning, it is necessary for the school to present, and for the students to approach, the Jewish heritage not as a museum, but as a living social force. It is, of course, imperative for the rabbinical schools to combat the ignorance about the Jewish past and to emphasize scholarship. But they must take care not to produce the type of young man described by Henry James as having become "so locked up in the past that he could not get back to his own era." The Jewish heritage is not meant to be primarily an object of delight to the heart of the antiquarian, philologist or bibliographer, nor even a thesaurus of texts for sermons. Nor can Jewish learning prove very fruitful if it is pursued in the spirit of those whom Solomon Schechter characterized as "studying engines." Our Sages long ago anticipated John Dewey in his emphasis upon the pragmatic aspect of all study. The well-known principle enunciated in *Avot* (I, 17), "Not study, but action is the important thing," is expressed in a multitude of dicta throughout the Rabbinic literature. *Unless the Jewish heritage can continue to function as a commitment and as an impelling drive to transform environment and condition men's inner lives and their relation to one another, there is no place for the rabbinic calling.* To function in that way, the Jewish heritage must be released from its state of dormancy. It must set in motion such forces in Jewish group life as will render that group life substantial and dynamic. It is this that prompted the great Palestinian Amora, R. Johanan, to declare that constructive social effort was the main task of the Jewish scholar. "The epithet 'builder,'" he said, "refers to the disciples of the wise, who throughout their entire life are engaged in the up-building of the world" (*Shabbat* 114a).

If Jewish life is not to be distilled to a residue of abstract ideals and memories stored away in books, the Jewish heritage should be presented to reveal the unconquerable sense of nation-hood which has survived all of Israel's vicissitudes, the social unity which, despite its lack of land and government, has pre-served the Jewish people as a nation. Those who regard nation-hood in terms of a social unit organized for power or combat will deny the Jews the right to call themselves a nation. But those who agree with Renan that the core of nationhood is not or-ganization for power, nor even the machinery of government, but a shared consciousness of a common past and the desire to have a common future, will concede that the Jews have never ceased to be a nation. It was the nationhood of the Jews that created and shaped their literature, their laws and folkways, their mores and religion.

How is this sense of nationhood to be kept alive in the Jews at the present time? What framework is shaping itself for Jewish unity throughout the world and for the local Jewries in each country? What is the significance of the modern Jewish renais-sance and of the rehabilitation of the Jewish homeland? All these questions the rabbi will have to answer, and his training should qualify him to answer without ambiguity or evasion. The rabbini-cal school should enable him to transmit the desire for a sub-stantial Jewish life, for Jewish communal organization and re-sponsibility, for Jewish customs and mores. The rabbi should make the maximum use of the vitalizing effect which reciprocal relations between diaspora and Israel exert upon Jewish life.

The survival of Judaism has become more dependent than ever upon its inherent power to transform itself. All ancient civilizations were markedly static. When we confine ourselves to the Judaism of a particular era, we get the impression that it too was immobile and chained to its own past. But if we include in our survey the whole of Judaism, we become aware of the power of self-transformation, the like of which no ancient culture pos-sessed. Only dynamic power of exceptional vigor could have enabled the Jewish people to remake itself from a henotheistic kingdom into a monotheistic commonwealth, and from a monotheistic commonwealth into an otherworldly theocracy. Such transformation in the case of any other people would have meant the substitution of one civilization for another. By some divine gift the Jewish people managed to bridge the gaps between the different stages of its history so that it did not experience the least break in the continuity of its life. Each crisis in its career brought about an adjustment which was creative of new spiritual values. The struggle against Canaanism elicited Prophetism. The effort to survive in the midst of a world politically and culturally subservient to Hellenism brought out in the Jews the Torah consciousness, with its apotheosis of the moral law. In striving to hold its own against a humanity obsessed with the desire to escape the responsibilities of this world, the Jews formulated a version of otherworldliness which was free from all tendencies to escape responsibility in the here and now. It is essential that those who want to guide Jews in the process of adjusting themselves to unprecedented conditions of life be thoroughly imbued with these dynamic and creative traits of the Jewish heritage.

To attain this intimate knowledge of Judaism, one must study it from within. The difference between getting one's knowledge of Judaism through the medium of its original language and getting that knowledge through translations is like the difference between being a participant in a game and being merely a spectator on the side lines. A rabbinic training should, therefore, qualify a student to go directly to the sources of Jewish information and prepare him to stem the general tendency of Jews in the diaspora to evade the effort involved in knowing and living Judaism from within. The ancient Rabbis had the right intuition when they said that "the day whereon the Bible was translated into Greek was as ominous as the day whereon the Israelites worshiped the Golden Calf" (*Soferim*, Ch. 1). They did not mean to decry the dissemination of the knowledge of the Bible. They merely deplored the fact that the Greek translation of the Bible had placed the large and important community of Jews of Alexandria outside the stream of Jewish life and caused them to be swept into the current either of Paganism or of Christianity. What happened to Alexandrian Jewry should serve as a warning to those who nowadays count upon the possibility of maintaining a Hebrew-less Judaism anywhere in the diaspora. The sterile values and bizarre aberrations which a translated Judaism yielded to a Philo of Alexandria, or to a Hermann Cohen of Germany, should discourage any lesser philosopher from attempting to effect a revaluation of Jewish values that is not rooted in a knowledge of Hebrew, both ancient and modern.

It is assumed that when a young man chooses the rabbinic calling, he comes, as a result of upbringing and home background, or perhaps of personal illumination, thoroughly imbued with the significance of religion and habituated in the outward expression of it. Rabbinical institutions are right in accepting as students only those who do not content themselves with merely believing in God, but who also appreciate the need of having the God consciousness interwoven with the daily life of the human being, incorporated in actions and symbols and articulated in prayer and worship. But they make the fatal mistake of believing that the momentum of the training and habituation in religious thought and practice acquired during the early years are sufficient to carry the student through years of the rabbinic training. The study of Bible and Talmud and Jewish philosophy, it is thought, will not only keep that momentum alive, but even reinforce it and prepare him adequately to meet the challenge of secularism and atheism when he assumes the duties of the ministry. In taking this attitude rabbinical training schools show themselves naive in their estimate of the forces that are shattering the traditional religious beliefs, a naiveté that is unworthy of institutions that undertake the responsibility of training spiritual leaders for our day.

The rabbi cannot afford to ensconce himself in the ivory tower of scholastic detachment and to declare the world to have gone insane with its new knowledge. He will find it hard enough to justify his calling in a materialistic and technologically oriented society. But if he will be an ignoramus in the philosophy, psychology and history of religion—subjects in which he of all people should be an expert—the contempt in which his office may be held will be justifiable. If the rabbinical student wants to contribute definite values to human life, he should give time and thought to the new disciplines in the study of religion. They have become indispensable to anyone who wants to get at the real issues behind the endless religious logomachies.

Men possessed "the peace that passeth understanding" as long as their understanding allowed for geocentrism, a manlike deity, supernaturalism and an otherworldly outlook. Mankind, especially Jewish mankind, would be grateful today for the least modicum of peace that is understandable. Of all peoples in the world, the Jews are the most disoriented religiously. Being city dwellers to a far greater degree than other elements of the population, they are in immediate touch with the latest conclusions in men's thinking. That thinking has certainly not helped the cause of religion. In proportion to their numbers, there is more dissatisfaction with, and revolt against, traditional religion among Jews than among Christians and Mohammedans. Organized religion is disestablished among Jews to a far greater degree than among non-Jews. Affiliation on the basis of religious belief is far below the general average of other peoples. Most disconcerting is the fact that very few, if any, of those Jews who figure prominently in the world of science, art or general achievement openly avow any interest in Jewish religion.

This present attitude toward religion—an attitude compounded of contempt based on prejudice, confusion in thinking and ignorance of facts—poses a challenge for the rabbi which he must face frankly and understandingly. He must be equipped with all that modern research has revealed concerning religion as an expression of human nature. The rabbinical schools should not permit their students to shift for themselves. It is not enough to teach what the ancient Jewish authorities had to say about God, Israel and Torah or how they reconciled tradition with the philosophy of their day. Each age must have its own theology. The theology for our day can no more be extemporized than were the theologies of the past. It must take into account not only the tested personal and social experience of our generation, but also the newly acquired knowledge about man and his world, which has been incorporated into the scientific and inductive study of religion. *The rabbi should not be a walking sarcophagus of dead ideas about religion, but an interpreter of the experiences of the inner and outer life in terms of religion that are understandable and relevant.*

A scientific and inductive knowledge of Jewish religion presupposes an objective study of the history of the Jewish religion from its beginnings down to our own day. It is as necessary to isolate and organize the religious aspect of the Jewish past as it was necessary to isolate from the literary heritage an ordered account of the vicissitudes of the Jewish people, which could be called history. It is less than a century since Jewish history has gained recognition as a subject of study in its own right. Similar recognition should now be accorded to the study of Jewish religion.

Such study should achieve a realistic account of the beginning and development of the Jewish religion down to our own day. Facts have a certain charm of their own. There are, of course, difficulties which beset a realistic account of Israel's beginnings, since you find biblical scholars denying the Exodus, the existence of Moses and even the distinction between Israelites and Canaanites. But the very knowledge that the dawn of Jewish religion is clouded in obscurity is not without its value. It can be utilized to transfer the emphasis from the phantasies which ancients wove about Israel's beginnings to the unmistakable miracle of the Jewish consciousness which wove those phantasies and to the significance of the design into which they were woven.

The inwardness of the religious experiences of those who shaped the religion of Israel has hardly been explored. Although the canonical prophets have recently been properly appraised, yet what they actually believed about God, how they communed with Him or how much of fact and how much of subjective interpretation there was in their religious insight are questions which have scarcely been formulated. Too little attention is paid to the part played by the priesthood in Israel, the class of men who effected the synthesis between the abstract ideals of the prophets and the inevitable elements of popular religion. They surely possessed a religious perspective worthy of being better known. How much do we know of the inner experiences of the Sages, whose wisdom corresponded to the practical wisdom enunciated by some of the foremost Greek philosophers? Why do we not delve into the soul of the Psalmists, whose intimate sense of Godhood inspired poetry which expressed the inexpressible? The doubt and despair voiced in Job and Koheleth represent a movement which meant the broadening of Jewish horizons and the heralding of a more realistic conception of God. An altogether new vista of religious experience opens up with the writings of the Apocrypha and Pseudepigrapha. When we come to the Rabbinic literature, we have valuable compendia of the ideology of the ancient Rabbis in Solomon Schechter's *Some Aspects of Rabbinic Theology* and George Foote Moore's *Judaism*. But Rabbinic religion as a phenomenon of the human soul—creating a complex of ideas which served as a wall to shut out intolerable realities, and as a social force both countering and interacting with hostile social forces—has not even been discovered.

This approach to the religious aspect of the Jewish past presupposes the study of religion as a manifestation of human nature, which calls for an appreciable knowledge of the religious experience of other peoples. It is not only necessary to know something about the religion of the Babylonians and the Egyptians, to have read W. Robertson Smith's *Semitic Origins*, Jane Harrison's *Themis*, W. Warde Fowler's *The Religious Experience of the Roman People* and Adolph Harnack's *Lehrbuch der Dogmengeschichte*, and works of a similar character, but also to bring to bear upon such knowledge the results of modern studies in the psychology of religion. This approach would emancipate the mind of the rabbinical student from provincial notions about religion and direct him toward the permanent human needs which religion seeks to meet. Only thus will he be able to distinguish between the transitory and the abiding in the various religious expressions of the human race.

Somehow there has arisen the notion that the psychological and comparative study of religion will undermine belief. The shock of learning facts which have hitherto been kept out of the sphere of religious knowledge, or were unknown, unsettles accepted beliefs and traditions. But shall we change the well-known biblical saying, "The fear of the Lord—or religion—is the beginning of wisdom," to read, "The fear of the Lord is the end of wisdom?" Nothing can be gained by the policy of self-protective ignorance. The medieval priest who refused to look into the telescope for fear that he might have to change his views about the physical universe could not prevent others from looking. Religion will continue to be studied from a comparative and psychological point of view. Why should not the schools that train men for the specific purpose of teaching religion take the lead in the scientific study of religion? Why should the most constructive religious thinkers have to find the field for their teaching not in the schools that train for the ministry, but in the universities and the colleges? It is, indeed, paradoxical that Jews who boast of having given the world the truest conception of God should have to fall back upon quotations from Jeans and Eddington to prove that there is a God.

Without a naturalist and humanist understanding of religion, it is impossible for anyone to have a correct idea of what is happening to religion today. If the rabbi who lacks such an understanding happens to be of a religious temperament, he will assume that his contemporaries are spiritually degenerate and will resort to scolding. He will fail to discern in the present-day movements and aspirations anything in common with traditional religion. He will spend himself in futile nostalgia for men's lost innocence and find himself unable to help his people in their religious maladjustments. Only a proper training in the study of religion will develop in him the ability to discern in the present mass of conflicting idealisms the particular element which is inherently continuous with the religious experience of the past. Men are as sincerely and earnestly groping toward the ideal of a better life as the most simple-celled organism naturally turns toward the sun. Heliotropism has its analogue in the domain of the spirit. The teacher of religion should evolve modern equivalents for the traditional religious values. With those equivalents he would be able to supply what is missing in the one-sided idealisms which reckon only with the basic needs of human life, but which fail to take human life as a whole into account. No social idealism can be adequate so long as it fails to recognize the very implications which underlie it and so long as it refuses to accept the universe as being in rapport with man's endeavors to make this world a better place to live in. It is the task of religion to make good this inadequacy.

No student should present himself as a candidate for the rabbinic calling unless he believes that the Jews as a people have developed an effective method of salvation and living, whereby the human being is most likely to fulfill himself and human society to attain its true purpose. To justify this assumption, a modern rabbinic training has so to enlarge the traditional conception of Torah as to make Torah synonymous with the life-long process of spiritual growth through education. Torah must come to mean the continuous study of human affairs and relationships, with a view to bringing them into line with the ethical purposes of life. The Torah can no longer be presented as a static system of laws whose rightness and finality are guaranteed by their supernatural origin. It must be translated into a process of education that would help the Jew attain a vitalizing and redeeming perspective on life, that would furnish him with a sense of values whereby he could distinguish not only between good and evil, but also between a lesser and a greater good and between a lesser and a greater evil, and that would point to the incentives necessary to impel us to live up to the dictates of our better judgments. The rabbi is essentially the teacher who, through the medium of the pulpit, organized instruction and personal influence, voices and demonstrates the possibilities for the salvation of mankind, which inhere in the process of moral and spiritual growth in accordance with the spirit of Torah.

Adult education, which is gradually attaining the proportions of a worldwide movement, is based on a philosophy which has much in common with the idea of Torah. That philosophy implies that the human being will never achieve the good life through a religion which confines itself to creedal assent, divorced from social duties and responsibilities. To discharge those duties and responsibilities the rabbi must apply his knowledge of the right to the concrete situations which constitute the substance of daily living.

A strange controversy has been raging within the American rabbinate. One party to the controversy charges the other, either outrightly or indirectly, with teaching a godless Judaism. It is conceivable that a rabbi who ceased to believe in God might be hypocritical enough to stay at his post. He might even thump his pulpit all the more forcibly to drown the inner voice of denial with loud protestations of belief. But that he could openly teach a godless Judaism is absurd. He might as well try to advocate an anti-Semitic Judaism. On the other hand, there is the all too familiar phenomenon of rabbis teaching a Torahless Judaism. To invoke the name of God and to sing His praises—making up for their monotony by a weekly homily adorned with glittering generalities—is to repeat the sin of ancient Israel, who, in common with all other peoples of the world, found it much easier to worship God than to obey His laws. To these self-appointed champions of God there comes the rebuke of our Sages who said, "Would that they had let God alone and did something with His Torah" (*Ekah Rabbati*, Ch. I).

The Jewish religious genius which spoke through the prophets discerned—in the shaping of human life in accordance with the ideas of "righteousness spelled into law"—a more effective demonstration of the reality of God than in elaborate ritual. The Pharisaic leaders and their successors, the Tannaim and Amoraim, were likewise true to the Jewish religious intuition when they resisted the attempt of various sectaries to substitute mystic faith for the study of Torah and obedience to its laws. *Now that the entire structure of the moral life is tottering, the problem is not to get men to believe in God, but to reconsruct their conception of God that they might realize once more the imperative character of the moral law.*

Men have become cynical in their attitude toward moral values because traditional religious conceptions are untenable. The belief in the supernatural origin of the moral laws and in the sanctions of reward and punishment to be meted out in this world or in the next has lost its hold on the majority of thinking men and women. Man needs not merely God, but God who is a giver of Torah.

Such a God has to be discerned through the emergent faith in the worth of human personality. The regenerative tendency in mankind is asserting itself in a deepened respect for that incommunicable and untransferable individuality in the human being which is the point of reference of everything that is sacred and beautiful. This growing awareness of the worth of personality as unconditioned by creed, race or nation, and as due to its latent possibilities for good, is revolutionizing human society. It is conferring rights upon the woman, the child, the disinherited, the oppressed. It is the inspiration behind the striving for equitable distributions of opportunities. By understanding fully all that is implied in human worth the Jew can gain deeper insight into his own spiritual heritage.

The exact equivalent of Torah, however, calls for something more than even the recovery of the basic principles underlying the consciousness of duty and of ethical law. It includes the application of ethical norms and sanctions to the specific relationships that exist between the sexes, between children and parents, youth and adult, buyer and seller, employer and employee, citizen and state, world and individual. Just now, the economic aspect of civilization occupies the center of attention. Modern industry with its new methods of production and distribution has rendered some of the traditional standards of justice inadequate. These new conditions call for a new conscience in matters economic. How shall such a conscience be developed? Certainly not by resorting to violence. For whatever is established by violence must be defended by force; and whatever has to be defended by force cannot come within the category of the moral. The only alternative to violence is a comprehensive educational process which shall encourage the open and frank discussion of all ethical problems involved in the exchange of goods and services.

Such education is not another name for the haphazard evolution which is usually depended upon to save us from violent revolution. It is rather a synonym for the directed, peaceful and accelerated development which must henceforth become part of human affairs if civilization is to be saved. Such education is in true line of succession to the spirit and method of Torah. It is evident that, for the rabbi to be capable of fostering such education, he will have to be sufficiently acquainted with the broad outlines of the modern social sciences. Burdensome as is the added responsibility of making the necessary provisions for the proper orientation of their students in the social sciences, the rabbinical schools dare not send forth as spiritual and ethical leaders men who are unprepared to throw light upon the conflicting interests of groups and individuals.

In the attempt to describe the spirit in which rabbinical students should approach their studies and the rabbinical schools train prospective rabbis, all reference to the various types of present-day Judaism has been deliberately omitted. Rabbinic students should be acquainted with the issues which divide the various groups among Jews and the philosophy of each group should be explained and interpreted. But the rabbinical school should eschew the type of indoctrination which goes with partisanship and the disparagement of the ideas and ideals of other trends.

With the foregoing program the only compatible method of interpreting the religious divisions among Jews is that which sees in those divisions various denominations within the social structure of the Jewish people. Jews are bound together by interests and purposes that far transcend the issues which divide them. Their underlying unity is implied in the belief in what Solomon Schechter spoke of as "catholic Israel." Such belief, however, must find expression in a catholicity of mind and of heart which can enable those who are fitting themselves for the rabbinate to appreciate the important contributions which each of the existing groups has made to Jewish life.

To the Orthodoxy of a Samson R. Hirsch and David Hoffman belongs the credit of accentuating the religious interpretation of life and the permeation of everything that the Jew does, with a sense of consecration. Reformism, as represented by Ludwig Geiger and Kaufmann Kohler, has rendered invaluable service in having indicated the need for adjusting Judaism to modern life. Conservatism, whose spokesmen were Zacharias Frankel and Solomon Schechter, has expressed the significant intuition that historic continuity is the principal criterion of the validity of any adjustment of Judaism to present-day needs. Nationalism, as taught by Ahad Ha-Am, Nahman Syrkin and Hayim Zhitlowsky, in placing social idealism at the center of

Jewish life, has come nearest to reproducing the prophetic emphasis upon the ethical implications of religion. In advocating the foregoing Jewish ecumenicity the Reconstructionist movement is giving expression to its conception of Judaism as an evolving religious civilization.

Any program which is to stimulate, direct and enrich Jewish life in this country will have to avoid the weakness and appropriate the strength of each of the existing Jewish ideologies. It was inevitable for the first reaction to the conditions created by the Emancipation and the Enlightenment to result in these four different conceptions of the future of Jewish life. It was equally inevitable for the institutions, which trained men for leadership in Jewish life under the stress of the first reaction, to commit their graduates to one or the other of these conceptions as the only one that is tenable and legitimate. It has now become necessary to retrieve that wholeness of Jewish life which is lacking in each of these conceptions. If there is to be a future to Jewish life, the Jews will have to achieve a synthesis of the insights and purposes which each of the existing groups has arrived at in its desire to perpetuate and fructify the Jewish heritage. That is the direction toward which the most constructive tendencies in contemporary Jewish life are moving. That is the meaning of the gradual effacement of the lines that at present divide the denominations. The rabbinical institutions will show the way to the next stage in Judaism, if they will guide their students in the direction of religious pluralism within Judaism.

Epilogue

Two spiritual eruptions of volcanic dimension took place in Jewish life during the twentieth century: the Holocaust of the gas chambers and the establishment of the State of Israel. The first rendered the traditional idea of God untenable; the second rendered the traditional conception of normative Judaism as limited to the Land of Israel unacceptable. Both events have brought Jewish life within the ambit of the modern age, which is different from all past ages in being an age of deliberately violent revolution instead of unconscious evolution.

Revolution implies a radical break with the past, a complete rejection of the cherished values, standards and ideals of the past. This revolution figures as communism in the politico-economic institutions, as utter shamelessness in literature, theater and sex relations, and as atheism in religion. Having begun toward the end of the eighteenth century, it has been accelerating ever since to the point of the most terrifying explosion in our day.

Unfortunately the human mind, as a whole, has not yet learned how to deal with an age of revolution. That is because it is still lacking in a most vital capacity, namely, the exercise of *social* forethought. To be able to deal with an unprecedented situation in human life, the human mind must possess sufficient imagination to foresee possible consequences of the attempt to deal with a crisis in one's affairs. Most people of high intelligence possess such imagination with regard to their own persons. Very few indeed, however, are self-aware of sharing the collective mind of the various organic societies to which they belong. They are therefore unable to envisage the consequences of whatever course of action an organic society in a state of crisis might decide to take.

As a result, in an age like ours the tendency of the members of an organic society like a nation or people is to divide themselves into rightists and leftists: into those who resist revolution and those who go along with it; into those who see no hope for the future except by holding on to the past, and those who foresee only the good in the new and the untried. In American Jewish life the tendency to resist cultural and spiritual revolution is strongly manifest in Orthodox, and less strongly manifest in Conservative, Judaism. On the other hand, the tendency to go along with revolution is strongly manifest in secular Judaism and less strongly manifest in Reform Judaism. Among the established nations the rivalry between these two conflicting tendencies prevents the advancement of social progress, but does in no way make for social disintegration. American Jewish life, however, which is subject to the centripetal pull of the vast majority population, is undergoing social disintegration. As a consequence there are three kinds of American Jews: drop-outs, drop-ins, and stay-ins, in the proportion, respectively, of about one-half, one-third and one-fourth, with the stay-ins moving toward the drop-ins and the drop-ins moving toward the drop-outs. The one superfluous twelfth may be accounted for by the "about."

The only way it would be possible to counteract that social disintegration of American Jewish life is to formulate an ideology concerning the humanizing function of the Jewish collective consciousness and a program of action for the reorganization of the Jewish social, religious and Zionist agencies, with a view to integrating them into *organic* Jewish communities. As for the program of action, enough has been said about it in the body of the book. The matter of new ideology, however, is specifically relevant to the method of evolutionary adjustment in an age of revolution.

Given the kind of individual self-awareness which is at the same time aware of sharing the collective mind of the organic society one belongs to, a third alternative is likely to present itself. For such a mind to reject the past *in toto* is to cut adrift from one's organic society and to forfeit one's sense of identity. To hang on to it at all costs is to repudiate one's own individuality. A third alternative therefore is to operate with the assumption that the most wholesome way of dealing with an age of revolution is by the method of evolutionary adjustment. That consists in conserving from the past whatever of intrinsic value transcends the vicissitudes of circumstance and synthesizing it with whatever in the present is of ultimate concern. That evolutionary method of adjustment as an onging process applied to the needs of the present situation in Jewish life resulted in the Reconstructionist conception of Judaism as an evolving religious civilization.

If traditional Judaism were merely a religion, it could hardly be regarded as identical with the religion of the Hebrew Bible, so wide a gap actually divides them. That is the gap in the conception of divine justice. Fundamental to the biblical conception of divine justice is that the rewards and punishments for human behavior are meted out in *this* world (cf. Jer. 9:23). The very existence of a hereafter world is never alluded to in the Hebrew Bible. That would be more than enough to make of the post-biblical Judaism a different religion from the religion of the Bible. Likewise, if modern Judaism were to treat the miracles of the Bible as mythology rather than as history, it could not be regarded as the same religion as that of the Bible. Only by viewing Judaism as a civilization, with religion as articulating its purpose and meaning, is it possible to identify the collective consciousness which is articulated and transmitted by means of a social heritage known as Torah—both written and oral (later also written).

Evidently the only way the Jewish civilization can be expected to function in our revolutionary age is to indicate wherein it is relevant to our most urgent concerns. It so happens that the most urgent concern is the abolition of war as a means of settling international disputes, since the atomic weaponry which would be used in war is certain to devastate the earth and render it uninhabitable. That necessitates the limitation of national sovereignties, and the submission to international courts for adjudication of all international disputes. Both these facts, in turn, presuppose the functioning of ethical nationhood by every nation individually.

With Judaism conceived as a civilization, we are in a position to study its religion for the purpose of identifying in it those aspirations which unmistakably foreshadow the urgent need in our day for ethical nationhood as a means to universal welfare and peace. Moreover, in addition to contributing to the purpose and meaning of Jewish life in our day, the conception of Judaism as a civilization does much to deepen the sense of greater reality to factors than to facts, since they create facts. Among such factors are values, collective consciousness and God. Those factors answer to man's awareness of his needs. That is of utmost significance with regard to the belief in and conception of God. Therein is the essential difference between the Hebraic and the Hellenic attitude toward the idea of God. Whereas to the Hebraic mind God is a factor that answers most particularly to man's spiritual needs for controlling and directing his efforts to satisfy his biological and psycho-social needs, to the Hellenic mind God is an answer to the logical demand for the cause of nature. As such, God is the "moveless mover." Contrast that virtually inconceivable idea of God with the idea of God expressed in the myth of Abraham and the three visitors, where God figures as functioning through "justice spelled out into law" (Gen. 18:19).

That the Hebraic conception of God as answering to man's needs is relevant to the ultimate concern of mankind for universal peace becomes apparent when we realize that there *can* be enough in the world to satisfy men's needs, but not to satisfy men's greeds for pleasure and power.